Practical KABBALAH
for MAGIC & PROTECTION

וְיֹאמְרוּ הַגּוֹיִם אַיֵּה־נָא אֱלֹהֵיהֶם: וֵאלֹהֵינוּ בַשָּׁמָיִם כֹּל אֲשֶׁר־חָפֵץ
עָשָׂה: עֲצַבֵּיהֶם כֶּסֶף וְזָהָב מַעֲשֵׂה יְדֵי אָדָם: פֶּה־לָהֶם וְלֹא יְדַבֵּרוּ עֵינַיִם
לָהֶם וְלֹא יִרְאוּ: אָזְנַיִם לָהֶם וְלֹא יִשְׁמָעוּ אַף לָהֶם וְלֹא יְרִיחוּן: יְדֵיהֶם
וְלֹא יְמִישׁוּן רַגְלֵיהֶם וְלֹא יְהַלֵּכוּ לֹא־יֶהְגּוּ בִּגְרוֹנָם: כְּמוֹהֶם יִהְיוּ עֹשֵׂיהֶם
כֹּל אֲשֶׁר־בֹּטֵחַ בָּהֶם: יִשְׂרָאֵל בְּטַח בַּיי עֶזְרָם וּמָגִנָּם הוּא: בֵּית אַהֲרֹן
בִּטְחוּ בַיי עֶזְרָם וּמָגִנָּם הוּא: יִרְאֵי יי בִּטְחוּ בַיי עֶזְרָם וּמָגִנָּם הוּא:
יי זְכָרָנוּ יְבָרֵךְ יְבָרֵךְ אֶת־בֵּית יִשְׂרָאֵל יְבָרֵךְ אֶת־בֵּית אַהֲרֹן: יְבָרֵךְ
יִרְאֵי יי הַקְּטַנִּים עִם־הַגְּדֹלִים: יֹסֵף יי עֲלֵיכֶם עֲלֵיכֶם וְעַל־בְּנֵיכֶם:
בְּרוּכִים אַתֶּם לַיי עֹשֵׂה שָׁמַיִם וָאָרֶץ: הַשָּׁמַיִם שָׁמַיִם לַיי וְהָאָרֶץ נָתַן
לִבְנֵי־אָדָם: לֹא הַמֵּתִים יְהַלְלוּ־יָהּ וְלֹא כָּל־יֹרְדֵי דוּמָה: וַאֲנַחְנוּ נְבָרֵךְ

Practical Kabbalah for Magic & Protection

Vanessa Lampert

FRIEDMAN/FAIRFAX

In memory of my father, Sidney Abraham Pepper, 1905–1991,
who taught me so much

A FRIEDMAN/FAIRFAX BOOK

Please visit our website: www.metrobooks.com

This edition published by Friedman/Fairfax by arrangement with
Cico Books Ltd

ISBN 1586635514

1 3 5 7 9 10 8 6 4 2

Distributed by Sterling Publishing Company, Inc.
387 Park Avenue South
New York, NY 10016
Distributed in Canada by Sterling Publishing Canadian Manda Group
One Atlantic Avenue, Suite 105
Toronto, Ontario, Canada M6K 3E7
Distributed in Australia by
Capricorn Link (Australia) Pty Ltd.
P.O. Box 704
Windsor, NSW 2756, Australia

Designed by David Forham
Illustrations by Jacqui Mair and Samantha Wilson
Printed and bound by Kyodo Printing, Singapore

Note
This book reflects the views of the author based on her knowledge and
experience of the subject, and therefore is not intended to represent the
many forms of Kabbalah and its teaching. It is not the wish nor intention
of the publisher or author to cause offence to any group or individual. If
any statement or implication gives offence, this is entirely unintentional.

Contents

WHAT IS KABBALAH?

The enlightened will shine like the brightness of the sky and those who
make the masses righteous will shine like the stars for ever and ever.

DANIEL 12.3

KABBALAH IS A simple and accurate method that examines and defines man's place in the universe. The wisdom found in Kabbalah explains and teaches us why we exist, why we are born, why we live, what is the purpose of our lives, where we come from, and where we are going after this lifetime.

Above: *Kabbalah translates from Hebrew as "received." The study of Kabbalah is called "the Hidden Wisdom."*

KABBALAH IS ABOUT reaching and opening ourselves up to the spiritual world. It teaches us about spirituality, and how, through study, we can become an open channel to the upper spiritual realms. It is neither an abstract nor a theoretical study, but it is a very practical one. Through studying and understanding Kabbalah, we will learn about ourselves, who we are, and why we are here. We will learn what we need to do to change ourselves step by step. All knowledge, experimentation, and heightened perception gained through the study of Kabbalah is very personal and takes place within ourselves, which is why it is called "The Hidden Wisdom." The changes are invisible to those around us, and are totally unique to each and every one of us. *Kabbalah* is a Hebrew word that means "received." It is the term that is applied to a vast body of esoteric knowledge and practice, and to find its origins we must look back to the beginning of the Jewish religion. From Judaism's earliest days, mystics and thinkers have sought to understand the real nature of God and the universe we live in. They understood that in order to try to achieve this, they must first of all understand the inner nature of the human psyche.

Although there are many thousands of Kabbalist texts in existence (and probably many thousands that have not survived), until comparatively recently the primary method of teaching Kabbalah has been through the means of oral tradition from teacher to disciple.

Anyone can become a Kabbalist, because it is a philosophical system, not a religion. It is a way of life that changes the way we look at the universe, and enhances our relationship with God. The ultimate purpose of Kabbalah is to make us an open channel that will allow us to communicate directly with God. In order to do this, we must undergo a spiritual metamorphosis, which will not only alter the way we do things and think, but will allow us to open up to understanding man's destiny and the workings of the cosmos.

One of the strengths of Kabbalah is that there are no defined perimeters as to how it can be studied or developed. Not only has each generation and every teacher developed their own meanings, definitions, and theories, but Kabbalah has also changed and grown with every generation since its beginnings, and will continue to do so in the future, to meet the spiritual needs of the people.

Even though until recently its complex and profound teachings were inaccessible to Western society, and were either secretly passed down orally or were written in the ancient languages of Aramaic and Hebrew, you will notice how many of its teachings and ideas have parallels in the spiritual traditions of the East. In fact, I feel that although I was brought up with traditional Judaic oral knowledge of Kabbalah, and then in my adulthood went on to study global spiritual beliefs, I have now returned to my roots of knowledge and found that everything that I have learned on the way is all available within Kabbalah—I have come full circle.

Like a diamond, there are many different facets and faces to the practice of Kabbalah. Not only have the teachings been handed down through the ages untouched and unchanged by rabbis, but there are now many branches of Kabbalah-based traditions that have very little to do with its Jewish roots.

Above and below: *The Hebrew letters Vav and Hei. In meditation (see pp. 151, 152), Hei is a focus for spiritual development, and Vav for self-expression and communication.*

7

Left: *The Star of David, began to be used as a Kabbalist amulet of protection around the twelfth century BCE.*

TRADITIONAL KABBALISTS DIVIDE THE NATURE OF KABBALAH INTO THREE TYPES:

THEORETICAL KABBALAH—this is the thinking man's Kabbalah, which grew out of the traditional routes of spending a lifetime studying, discussing, and theorizing the underlying meanings of holy texts and writings. It concerns the dynamics of how God reveals Himself through different channels of spirituality and reality, theories of creation and the cosmos, and of the nature of man.

MEDITATIVE KABBALAH explores how mankind can connect with God, and what channels can be used. This is usually done through meditation and prayer.

PRACTICAL KABBALAH is the more spiritual aspect and probably the most widely recognizable to most people. The study of Practical Kabbalah is designed to bring about practical, self-help programs that we can easily recognize. This form of Kabbalah also encourages the more "magical" aspects of study, and from it stems a whole range of everyday beliefs and practice.

Above: *Red ribbon or pure red wool is one of the most well-known amulets of protection against the evil eye (see p. 64).*

correspondences about the Paths of the Tree of Life, which they based on the very ancient, but hitherto neglected Kabbalist text, the *Sepher Yetzirah* (Book of Creation).

THE WESTERN MYSTERY TRADITION developed from several modern schools of thought that evolved from the Golden Dawn, and especially its later members Aleister Crowley (1875–1947) and Dion Fortune (born Violet Firth, 1891–1946). It is from here that we get the various spellings of Kabbalah, such as Quabalah, Qabalah, and Cabalah, that often refer to the more magical and occult offshoots of the traditions. Aleister Crowley and his followers emphasized this magical aspect, while Dion Fortune is best remembered for her book, *The Mystical Qabalah*, which intertwines her knowledge of occult Kabbalah with her keen understanding of psychology. It is also from this tradition that we get the links between Kabbalah and Tarot.

THESE FORMS OF KABBALAH FORM THE BASIS OF LATER, MORE WESTERNIZED FORMS OF STUDY AND PRACTICE, WITH WHICH MANY ARE FAMILIAR TODAY.

CHRISTIAN KABBALAH began to grow in Medieval times, when versions of some ancient Hebrew and Aramaic writings were translated into Latin. Although the original motive for this was that by using Kabbalist arguments the Jews would convert to Christianity, in fact it led to an interest by Christians, who saw in the writings much that made sense to them in understanding their own faith. Ceremonial magicians were fond of appropriating Kabbalistic words of power, and by the late fifteenth and sixteenth centuries Western Kabbalists were augmenting the Kabbalah with aspects of Christian theology. By the seventeenth century, the time of the Enlightenment, the growing traditions of Freemasonry, Templarism, Alchemy, and Rosicrucianism had become profoundly influenced by Kabbalah.

THE HERMETIC ORDER OF THE GOLDEN DAWN was founded in London in 1888 by Dr. William Wynn Westcott (1848–1925) and Samuel Liddell Macgregor Mathers (1854–1918). Together, with the adaptation of the Kabbalah by the French occultist Eliphas Levi (1810–75), they used the basics of Kabbalah to form a coherent system in its own right. This group described itself as a Hermetic Order, and although many of its members were from Rosicrucian and Freemasonry backgrounds, its traditions were firmly based on Alchemy. This order kept alive the interest in Practical Kabbalah at a time when Jewish interest in mysticism was waning. It developed an elaborate system of

PRESENT TRENDS – in the last few years the study of Kabbalah has undergone a new metamorphosis, as it attracts not only liberal Jews and Christians, who might have in the past looked to Eastern philosophies for their spiritual solace. Many people now call Kabbalah the "Yoga of the West." Media stars are now photographed proudly displaying their red woolen bracelets and proclaiming how Kabbalah has changed their lives. Many centers around the world are now teaching how learning Kabbalah can lead to self-fulfillment, peace of mind, and contentment.

From an esoteric viewpoint, I firmly believe that this interest and spread of what was always a hidden knowledge is firm proof that the world is spiritually going through a profound change. What was and is probably the oldest spiritual tradition in the world has suddenly come to the forefront to spearhead the spread and adherence to looking at our relationship with God, the cosmos, ourselves, and mankind.

Above: *Aramaic writing is the precursor of Hebrew; it is shown here with Stars of David.*

A Brief History

THE ROOTS OF Kabbalah are lost in the mystery of time, but many believe that Adam and Noah were fully aware of Kabbalist teachings. It was Abraham who wrote down what is probably the earliest major Kabbalist text, the *Sepher Yetzirah*, or *Book of Creation*. Legend has it that at the age of forty-eight Abraham, already an acclaimed astrologer, began to reflect on the connection between the one true God and the universe, and after studying for three years he became so wise that he composed the *Sepher Yetzirah*. This book explores the connection between numbers, letters, sounds, the Zodiac, and the ten Sephirot with God and the cosmos.

The Jewish nation went into exile in 586 BCE to Babylon after the destruction of the First Temple, and there they were greatly influenced by magical beliefs and superstitions. Upon their return, the Israelites incorporated this mysticism, together with other influences from their neighboring lands, in religious pluralism—syncretism (the free combining of beliefs and practices from a number of spiritual traditions), apocalypse (speculations on the heavenly realms, angels, creation, and the end of history), and gnosticism (the attempt to transcend the material world and reach a true understanding of God).

From this melting pot of trends, there developed the practice known as *Maaseh Merkavah*, "The Matter of the Chariot," based on the chariot vision

in Ezekiel 1, which formulated a whole range of mystical and meditative practices. Practitioners would study the Bible and Jewish Law while maintaining moral and ritual purity in order to embark on inner meditative journeys through seven heavenly halls (*Hekhalot*) in order to attain an ecstatic vision of God's glory.

The first golden age of Kabbalah as a study in its own right did not occur until 1176, when the text known as *Sepher Ha-Bahir* (*Book of Brightness*) was published in Provence. This work discusses the esoteric meanings of biblical verses, the power of the Hebrew alphabet, the concept of the ten emanations or Sephirot of God, and reincarnation. Soon afterwards, in around 1200, also in Provence, Rabbi Isaac the Blind taught a small band of followers the connection between the Sephirot with meditation and prayer.

This was followed by the publication in the thirteenth century of *Sepher Ha-Zohar* (*Book of Splendor*) by Moses de Leon (c1240–1305) of Guadalajara, Spain, although many attributed its authorship to a second-century Galilean sage, Simeon bar Yohai. By weaving historical fact with myth, this book attempts to explain the origins of the beliefs of Kabbalah. It takes us through the ten Sephirot emanating from God and their individual natures, seen as both expressions of the nature of divinity, and as archetypes for all of creation. The expulsion of the Jews from Spain in 1492 helped spread the knowledge of the *Zohar* throughout Europe.

The second golden age of Kabbalah began in the mid-sixteenth century in Safed (in present-day Israel) by the followers of Rabbi Isaac Luria Ashkenazi (1534–72), known as the Ari, which became known as Lurianic Kabbalah. This charismatic teacher developed the first fully comprehensive system of study focusing on God's initial self-development, the creation of the cosmos and mankind, the origins of evil, and methods for repairing this evil (*Tikkun*) in order to restore the original unity of God and creation. In fact many of his methods of mediation and ritual for connecting man with God are still used today.

The downfall of the popularity of Lurianic teachings began in 1665, when a Turkish Jew, Shabbetai Tzvi (1626–76), who was fully immersed in

Above: *(From right) the Hebrew letters Beit (meaning at home in the cosmos); Gimel (kindness), and Daled (spiritual doorways).*

Below: *The chalice or cup represents love and receptiveness as a suit symbol of the Tarot, which is linked to Kabbalist tradition (see Divination and Occult Kabbalah, p. 122).*

Kabbalist teachings, pronounced himself the Messiah. Although many rabbis urged caution, Jews throughout Europe and the Near East became followers of this new school of mystical thought. In fact, many sold their possessions and had their bags packed ready to follow his call to follow him to Israel to rebuild the Temple. When Shabbetai and his followers reached Constantinople, the Sultan, fearing an uprising, imprisoned him. In 1666, upon being offered the choice between conversion to Islam or death, Shabbetai chose conversion. This betrayal, as it was thought, led to a period of great disappointment and negativity, which confined the elements of creativity and spread of Kabbalah.

It was not until Israel ben Eliezar (c.1700–60), known as the Baal Shem Tov, founded the Hassidic movement that there was a revival in the study and spread of Kabbalah. The Hassidic movement encouraged the unlearned Jew to see God in everything, and to practice a simple devotion in prayer, accompanied by singing, dancing, movement, and storytelling. The main problem was that the traditional rabbis, the Mitnaggdim (opponents), opposed these early Hassidim for their ecstatic and unscholarly ways, which led to many Hassidim eventually de-emphasizing their meditative practices and mystical teachings, thus leading to a more common ground between the two schools of thought.

The decline of mysticism throughout the nineteenth and early twentieth centuries began with the Reform movement in the West, which embraced pragmatism and sought social integration; the early Reform movements in Germany and North America removed anything faintly mystical from their prayer books. In eastern Europe, generations of Jews were annihilated by the Holocaust, and the heritage of Kabbalah was dealt a near-fatal blow. This period saw the English schools of mystical thought, such as the Golden Dawn, keeping alive the teachings of the Kabbalah. In the 1920s, Gershom Scholem (1897–1982) founded the first serious academic program in Jewish mysticism at the Hebrew University in Jerusalem.

The late 1960s saw things slowly changing, as a new generation of teachers began to infuse their congregations with their knowledge of Kabbalah. Feminist movements grew up and encouraged equal participation in Jewish mystical communities. And suddenly Jews who had been looking outside their religious confines to Eastern philosophies, such as Buddhism, suddenly began to realize that in Kabbalah there is a form of mystical practice equal to anything found outside Judaism.

Below: *The Hebrew letters Aleph (top) and Lamed (below).*

In the 1990s, Kabbalah was suddenly everywhere. It was no longer confined to the religious or to those involved with the more magical elements, but was practiced by people from every kind of religious background or belief in spirituality. And today Kabbalah is no longer a secret but is full of devotees who are suddenly discovering for themselves that Kabbalah is an all-encompassing philosophical system that teaches us not only how to explore the relationship between God, the cosmos, and ourselves, but also reveals to us the purpose of our existence.

Above: *Kabbalah is the study and practice of a philosophical system that explains our connection with God and the cosmos.*

What Kabbalah Can Do for You

A S WE HAVE SEEN, the word Kabbalah means "received tradition," and the question you must be asking yourself is "Receive what?"

Most of us, if asked to make a top ten list of what we would like to achieve, would include the following:

- **HEALTH**
- **HAPPINESS**
- **CONTENTMENT**
- **FREEDOM FROM STRESS**
- **LOVE AND RELATIONSHIPS**
- **FINANCIAL SECURITY**
- **PEACE OF MIND**
- **KNOWLEDGE**
- **SPIRITUAL ENLIGHTENMENT**
- **CONTROL OF DESTINY**

Above: *The sun relates to Tiferet, the sixth Sephirot on the Tree of Life (see pp. 30, and 132), a symbol central to Kabbalah.*

Below: *The Hebrew letter Kaph, which relates to willpower and awareness.*

By STUDYING KABBALAH, you will learn how to receive spiritual light and, with practice, achieve all of the above. You will learn through the development of your spiritual senses—often referred to as the sixth sense—how to understand yourself better, and how to tune into the true nature of the cosmos.

Our understanding of the true nature of the cosmos is limited by our five senses. According to the *Zohar*, each one of us is blindfolded because of the limitation of the information that filters through these five senses. An example of this is the radio: you switch it on and hear music, but you do not see the radio waves. Because you do not see them, it does not mean that they do not exist. If someone had written seventy-five years ago about the Internet, that information highway out there in cyberspace, people would have thought that they were probably crazy, or had a vivid imagination.

Through the Kabbalist teachings of meditation, contemplation, and the development of our spiritual inner selves, you will learn to understand things that are beyond our everyday senses. Kabbalists do not convey their knowledge of the structure of the upper worlds, or of the spiritual world, without reason. The important key that is found in their writings is that everybody has the ability to develop the sixth sense, and only after acquiring the sixth sense through study do we begin to see and feel a whole new purpose to our lives.

Kabbalists talk of "letting in the light," and by this we will learn through Kabbalah to allow the divine light of God into our hearts. The word "light" is considered by many Kabbalists to be a code word, a metaphor used originally some four thousand years ago to give us a glimpse into the essence and nature of the infinite energy force called God.

To try to better understand this, the example of the light and the vessel is introduced into many Kabbalist teachings. The light (God), created an infinite vessel to receive its endless good and its infinite nature of sharing. A simple example of this would be to think of a glass—the vessel—receiving and containing water—the light. The water is fulfilling the purpose of the glass, and the glass's purpose is to receive the water.

In order to become the vessel in this example, we must learn how to receive the light. First we must desire the light and fulfillment to enter our lives, and when it does we must be fully open to the energies of the divine, and allow it to correct us and guide us.

We must aim to become an open channel that is in alignment with the cosmos. Through Kabbalah we invoke the divine light to help us understand what we study, and to enter us. Through the practice of meditation this is our aim, and when we return out of the meditative state we remember what we felt, and try to keep that wonderful feeling with us as long as possible. Eventually, through practice, we will find our inner being transforming as we become more like the light we invoke. We will find ourselves automatically working with and tuning into the sixth spiritual sense, the spiritual vessel or *kli*, which will continue on its spiritual journey when our earthly body runs its course and perishes.

Kabbalah will teach you how to open up to spirituality that will totally change the way that you see and feel about things. It will also give your life a new purpose, and you will find yourself mentally elevated beyond materialism and mundane living.

The worldly focus on studying Kabbalah at this present time has an ultimate purpose. Mankind is on a preordained course of spiritual evolvement, and the popularity of Kabbalah is speeding up this spiritual

Above: *Water is a symbol of light, the energy-essence of God. Through the study of Kabbalah we become the vessel, ready to receive this divine light.*

Above, left: *Meditate on the letter Yod (top) to bring change. A Tet (below) meditation (see p. 152) helps you to recognize hidden goodness.*

Above: *The letter Chet (top) and Zayin (below). Meditate on Chet for better health, and on Zayin for less stress.*

metamorphosis. When we study Kabbalah, we not only begin to change and evolve as individuals – which affects the whole human consciousness – but we are also lifting the soul group of our generation onto a whole new level of spirituality.

Spirituality and Kabbalah

MOST OF US need a purpose in order to change our lives. We go to the gym to get fit, we go to the hairdresser to make our hair look good. Sometimes these changes can have an immediate effect, and sometimes they take longer. The point is that it is human nature that if we do not foresee a result and therefore a satisfaction from our actions, we call a halt.

Kabbalah teaches us how to receive. The end result that we are searching for is to attain spirituality. However, we must first work at it and expand our desire to receive:

• We must expand our will to absorb and understand all worlds, including this one.

• We must expand our will to understand, and work with our inner selves to absorb the changes that will change our ideas, attitudes, and, eventually, our lives.

IN ORDER TO START this change, we must first understand that this is the purpose that we are here for. In order to effect this change, we will not have to give anything up but just work a little harder on our inner selves.

Many of you reading this book may have never had any spiritual feelings before, but something has drawn you to this point. You have already begun

the learning process. Others reading this book are already on their preordained path to spiritual growth. The first part of learning Kabbalah is with the aid of your intellect, which will open up your heart and will help you to feel what is, and what is not, right for you. By opening up your heart you will be drawn naturally to the right decisions and actions for your spiritual growth.

Take your time reading this book, as Kabbalists teach that spirituality should be taught in small doses to all students to expand their will to receive ever more light and spiritual awareness. As you begin to absorb the energy, so you will gain greater depth, understanding, and fulfillment. With practice you will be able to reach the highest level of spirituality as you learn to connect through your soul with your Creator.

Kabbalah and Reincarnation

KABBALAH TEACHES US that none of us are new souls, and that we have all accumulated experiences from previous lives in other incarnations. Very much in keeping with the Eastern philosophy of Karma, it is taught that our souls return time and time again, in order to learn in each lifetime, and to eventually accomplish our ultimate spiritual destiny.

The number of souls is not infinite, and they return time and time again to learn their preordained lessons; each time they return in a different physical body, but the types of souls that are reborn are different. This is known to many cultures as reincarnation, but Kabbalists use another term, the development of generations. They also refer to it as *gilgulim*, which means the transmigration of the soul.

We are taught that the body is just the case, the package, that contains the soul, which is the essential part of our being. Whereas the "body" can be, and is, replaced, the soul returns each lifetime with the added experience and knowledge of its previous life here. It will also return with a renewed vitality that it has obtained while in heaven.

Above: *(From right) the Hebrew letters Ayin, meaning "eyes," Pei , or "mouth," and Tzaddi, meaning "righteous."*

Each generation of souls is distinct from the previous one, setting out to achieve different goals and desires. This leads to each "soul" generation developing and progressing along many different avenues of development. Some generations suffer more than others, such as those wiped out in the Holocaust, but to many Kabbalists and rabbis this is the way of that particular generation making progress and gaining experience toward their further development.

Each time a soul is reincarnated, it unconsciously seeks to understand its existence. Some souls are more developed than others, and it is these that actively seek out the truth and find that they want to look beyond the limitations of their five senses. They go out of their way to find the tools, books, learning aids, and teachers that help them understand and work within the spiritual world.

As the different soul groups descend, they need the best guidance available during that time period. This is why in every generation there will always be people who use the best methods of conveying knowledge available at that time. In this generation we have books, television, radio, workshops, and the Internet. In fact, we are part of a highly developed soul generation where there is an explosion of souls actively seeking knowledge. Never before has this been so easily available to so many. Never before has the interest in all things spiritual been so acceptable. It is also very easy to see how the generations of children born now are becoming more and more spiritually aware and developed.

In the Beginning God Created the Heavens and the Earth (the divine ray of light)

> The universe was created out of nothingness from a single point of
> light. This nothingness is called the Endless. The Endless was filled
> with infinite Light. The Light was then restricted to a single point,
> creating primordial space. Beyond this point nothing is known.
> Therefore the point is called "the beginning." After the Restriction, the
> Endless issued forth a ray of Light (energy). This ray of Light then
> expanded rapidly. All matter then emanated from that point.
>
> Isaac Luria

BEFORE TIME BEGAN and our universe exploded into being, the only thing
in existence was an infinite, unlimited force of pure energy—God. This
absolute force of energy was the only reality.

In order to explain the formation of the universe, Kabbalah teaches us the
concept of the *Three Negative Veils of Existence*. In order to understand the
universe and our place and purpose in it, we must first try to understand the
sequence of events that led to our existence.

God is the infinite absolute. Therefore the outermost veil is called AIN,
which translated means "nothingness." Nothing is relative to something, but
AIN is beyond both. This illustrates that God is neither above nor below, in
stillness nor in movement. God is beyond existence.

God wishes to perceive Himself, and because he had no point of
reference against which to compare, He created the universe. But first, He
had to create space—a void—in which the universe could exist. This is the
middle veil, the AIN SOPH, meaning "limitless without end." The oral
tradition of Kabbalah explains that the reasons for mankind's existence is
that "God wished to behold God," and so, where there had previously been
nothing, God withdrew a portion of Himself, thus creating an empty

19

space—a bubble—within this pre-existing vacuum state. God filled this bubble with a void in which a mirror of His existence could appear. This act is called *zimzum*.

Because there is no such thing as existence without God, so the divine light of God entered this bubble, and it was filled with His divinity. This act of creation is described in Genesis 1.3: God said "Let there be light." By this very act, God recognized His own existence and thereby also the existence of His supreme will. It also is our first demonstration of how words are used to carry out God's will. It is this act that first teaches us the power of words as tools, which is paramount to most branches of Kabbalah.

The innermost veil, which forms our conceptions of deity and universe, is called AIN SOPH AUR, "meaning without end." It is the combination of the AIN and AIN SOPH that formulates the AIN SOPH AUR. This concept attempts to convey the idea of a happening that is beyond the understanding of the human mind. AIN, AIN SOPH, and AIN SOPH AUR can be likened to states of cosmic unconsciousness. The three veils represent God before He becomes aware of Himself.

Below: *In Hebrew, the letter Samekh represents completion.*

Science describes this period of unmanifest existence, before the universe as we know it came into being, as the time before the Big Bang. The next stage, when from a single point an explosion of force produces the universe and its galaxies, is called the Big Bang. In Kabbalistic terms, this is the point that describes the coming-into-manifestation of God from the realms of the unmanifest. Although physics lacks the means to understand the spiritual significance of how and why the Big Bang occurred, the similarities of the two descriptions of the birth of the universe are uncanny.

"And there was light: and God saw that the light was good." Kabbalah teaches us that then God created the universe and every living thing, each of which contains within its being a blueprint of God's light and love.

"Then God said 'Let us make man in our image and likeness.'" (Genesis 1:26) It is from these words that we see the Kabbalist development of the

Above: *Star of David motifs are found throughout Kabbalist works.*

theory of the primordial Adam, called Adam Kadmon, who was created by the *kav*, the ray of divine light. Its emanation took part in two stages, the first in the form of ten rays of energy, and the second of a "manlike" being who encompassed these ten rays of energy.

Adam Kadmon is seen as a creation of pure divine light possessing ten vessels of pure energy, which we call *Sephirot*. From his abode in the highest world, Adam Kadmon is instrumental in not only the emanation of the Sephirot, but also in their reconstruction and repair.

This image of the Universe is also represented by the *Tree of Life*, which represents the creation of the universe, everything in it, and ourselves. Emerging from the first emanation of the AIN SOPH AUR is the bridge between negative existence and existence itself. This is known as EHYEH ASHER EHYEH—I AM THAT I AM, or, literally, "What will be, will be."

EHYEH ASHER EHYEH

I AM THAT I AM

Right: *The Hebrew letter Nun, associated with fertility.*

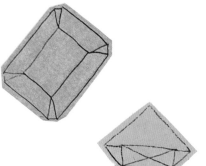

THE SEPHIROT: VORTEXES OF ENERGY

ACCORDING TO KABBALAH, as the AIN SOPH unloaded its energy into what we call the universe through the different stages, each successive level became more dense than the previous one. The energy, which had come from nothingness, acquired more and more substance with each progressive layer. The energy that came forth followed a pattern of emanation, limitation, expansion, until at last the energies solidified. The tenth and last level of emanation resulted in the universe that we are familiar with.

To understand how the Sephirot work, imagine that you are a swirling vortex of spiritual energies—these are the spiritual flows of the ten Sephirot, which are the building blocks of the cosmos and our individual personalities. This spiritual energy eventually manifests to become mind (*seichel*) and emotions (*middot*). The soul (*neshama*) is the channel through which the energy from these sources flows to animate our very being.

The word "Sephirot" has many meanings in Hebrew, including "sparkling lights," "sapphires," and "spheres of light," all of which try to describe a state of being, a world to which life and humanity aspire.

THE LIGHTNING FLASH

THE SEPHIROT ARE SAID TO have been formed from the divine by means of a Lightning Flash cutting through the veils of existence, instantly creating the manifest universe in a descending current of energy. Modern Kabbalists relate this to the moment of creation, the Big Bang.

Traditionally, it was thought that once the process of creation began, it was completed within seven days. We now know that these "days" were in fact periods of millions of years—a long time in comparison

> **The ten ineffable Sephirot have the appearance of the Lightning Flash, their origin is unseen, and no end is perceived.**
>
> *SEPHER YETZIRAH*

to the history of humanity, but probably no more than seconds or minutes to the Creator.

The zigzagging of the Flash, its first formulated Keter and then the following nine spheres, gives rise to the three vertical alignments in the Tree of Life, known as the Pillars.

Above: *Mem denotes a learned teacher and also a spirit guide.*

THE LIGHTNING FLASH & SEPHIROT

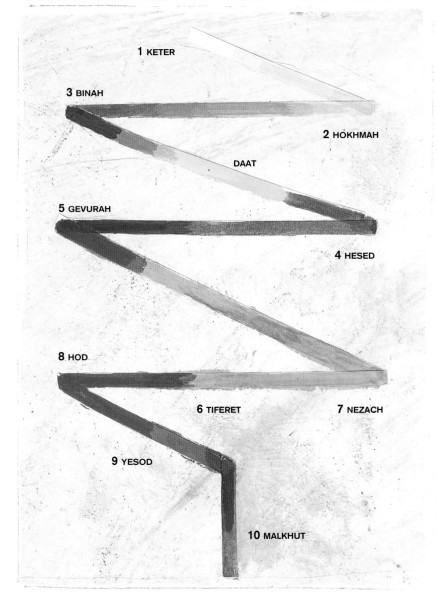

1 KETER

3 BINAH

2 HOKHMAH

DAAT

5 GEVURAH

4 HESED

8 HOD

6 TIFERET

7 NEZACH

9 YESOD

10 MALKHUT

Left: *The Lightning Flash expresses the process of the creation of each Sephirot and therefore the universe.*

Above: *Aleph (top) and Daled (below).*

THE FOUR WORLDS

EMERGING FROM THE first emanation of the AIN SOPH AUR is the bridge between negative existence and existence itself. This is called EHYEH ASHER EHYEH—which translates as I AM THAT I AM; it is commonly, interpreted as WHAT WILL BE, WILL BE.

Through the bridge of EHYEH ASHER EHYEH, God reveals Himself within existence. It is through the manifestation of the ten Sephirot into the first Tree of Life that the World of Atzilut came into being. Emerging from the AIN SOPH AUR, God's will came out of concealment into a state of existence. This point of emanation is the bridge between negative existence and existence itself.

The Hebrew word *olamot* means "worlds," and although most Kabbalists talk about the Four Worlds, and demonstrate this with illustrations of four basic realms, in truth the number is infinite.

The easiest way to imagine the Sephirot passing through the Four Worlds is to think of ten rays of creative light that are passing through four different layers, each occupying its own spiritual space. As these ten rays pass through each separate layer, their qualities change so that they become the "creatures" of that realm.

Each of these worlds can be considered as an independent hierarchy, each containing its own full Tree of Life. As our ultimate human manifestations take place in the final realm of Assiya, the person you are is determined by the Sephirot in the realm of Assiya.

Because of the fourfold aspect in each of the Four Worlds by each Sephirah, it becomes easy to apply Kabbalah to other systems, such as the Western elements of fire, air, water, and earth (see the illustration on the page opposite); Taoist diagrams, the letters of the Tetragrammaton (the Hebrew Name of God: YHVH), and in the Tarot deck, the cards of the Major Arcana (see page 124).

Opposite page: *The four elements of fire, air, water, and earth, link with the Four Worlds of the Sephirot on the Tree of Life.*

ATZILUT	The Divine Will	FIRE
BERIYA	The World of Creation (spirituality)	AIR
YETZIRA	The World of Formation (emotion)	WATER
ASSIYA	The World of Manifest (time, space, and earthly consciousness)	EARTH

ATZILUT The realm of Atzilut is closest to the divine source of God, and is indistinguishable from the light of infinity (AIN SOPH AUR), which is a metaphor for God—the light of the One who is infinite. It contains the first and highest manifestation of the ten Sephirot, then splits off into four levels that generate the appearance of the three lower level worlds of Beriya, Yetzira, and Assiya.

BERIYA This is the manifest world described in Genesis. It corresponds to the seven days of creation, and is home to the angelic realms. This world is guarded by the angel Metatron, and it is the bridge between Atzilut, which is the upper world of formation, and Yetzira, the lower world of formation.

YETZIRA The highest point of Yetzira reaches into the lowest point of the preceding world of Beriya. This world is less ethereal than the home of the angelic hosts, and is therefore more accessible to mankind. It corresponds to the Garden of Eden, and is the point of human interaction before Adam's descent into the world of Assiya.

ASSIYA This represents our world of matter. It also contains the realm of "shells" (klippot), where there are unbalanced energies that emerged from the primordial forms when God contracted the divine light to create the world.

It does not matter whether you choose to ascend or descend along the branches of the Tree of Life—the goal is to dissolve the ego and become as one with the AIN SOPH: to become an open channel with God.

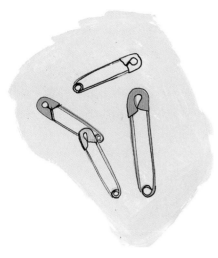

Left: *In our pre-existence, we progress through the Four Worlds before birth. Many rituals protect the soul of a new-born baby (see p. 64). Metal has protective power, which is why carrying safety pins prevails today. Pinning red ribbon on a baby's diaper or underclothing is another popular ritual.*

The Moment of Our Birth

KABBALAH TEACHES US that each and every one of us was present in the primordial body of Adam Kadmon, and therefore was in existence before Creation began. It was the act of Creation that was the source for our individual destiny.

Once the Four Worlds came into being, the divine part of each human entity divided into individual cells residing within the world of Beriya (Creation). We existed within this realm until we were called to Paradise, where our soul, which encompassed the Divine spark of Atzilut (Divine Will), took on a Yetziratic form (Formation) in order to be incarnated in the physical world of Assiya.

When this time came we appeared before God, who instructed each and every one of us in what our physical life journey was to accomplish—our

Top left: *Meditating on the Hebrew letter Resh enhances intuition. Meditating on Kuf (below left) is thought to boost knowledge.*

Right: *A modern rendition of the Lightning Flash.*

destiny. Although many were reluctant to descend into what one Kabbalist called this "vale of tears," the answer was "It was for this you were called, created, formed, and made."

It is said that when a couple are copulating the unseen soul of their future child is poised above them, and when conception occurs this soul becomes attached to the embryonic Assiyatic body of the world of earthly consciousness. As the foetus develops, so the soul who is to be incarnated is shown its future physical life, what lessons and journeys it will learn and travel, and the people it will encounter.

At birth, this prenatal knowledge is forgotten as the soul forgets about being a part of the upper worlds, and the baby becomes only aware of its physical life. However, occasionally a pre-natal memory may be dimly recalled, which is why sometimes when two complete strangers meet who have been acquainted in the spiritual realms, they have a feeling of déjà vu, familiarity, or they experience that special something that makes you aware that you are soul-mates.

In order to be born into the physical world of Assiya, our souls have descended through the Four Worlds and through the Lightning Flash of the Sephirot. As we mature, it is up to us to begin the descent back up through the Four Worlds until we accomplish our spiritual destiny. This re-learning process is accomplished by embarking on a spiritual journey that will lead us back up through the Lightning Flash in reverse.

Above: *Before we are incarnated in an earthly realm, we inhabit the world of Beriya (Creation), then Paradise.*

> Ten is the number of the ineffable Sephirot, ten and not nine, ten and not eleven. Understand this wisdom and be wise in the perception.
>
> SEPHER YETZIRAH

> When the twenty-two pathways and the ten Sephirot are combined, they comprise the thirty-two.
>
> PATHS OF WISDOM

> With thirty-two mystical paths of Wisdom engraved Yah, the Lord of Hosts, the God of Israel, the Living God, King of the Universe.
>
> SEPHER YETZIRAH

SOME OF THE earliest drawings of the Tree of Life date from those devised by Kabbalists in Medieval Spain and Provence. Further important schemes, commonly known as the Lurianic system, were based on the work of Isaac Luria, who lived and taught in Safed in sixteenth-century Palestine.

The diagram of the Tree can be seen to represent the physical, psychological, and spiritual components of humanity. It is composed of the ten Sephirot (singular, Sephirah) and twenty-two paths that connect them. The Sephirot are variously translated as emanations, worlds, spheres, and stages of consciousness.

The Sephirot as laid out in the Tree embody the stages of creation from the first emanations from God, reaching from the lowliest created object all the way up to the AIN SOPH. Every Sephirah is linked so that by starting at any point on the Tree, the spiritual seeker can eventually locate all the way up to the source.

All the Sephirot originally emanate from the Creator in the nonmanifest aspect, AIN SOPH, and His divine energy flows through all of the Sephirot like crystal-clear water. However, as this energy flows through each individual Sephirah, it also takes on various colors and forms of the material world.

The Tree is usually arranged in three distinct columns. The left-hand column, known as the *Pillar of Judgment*, is considered to have feminine,

Below: *The Hebrew letter Vav.*

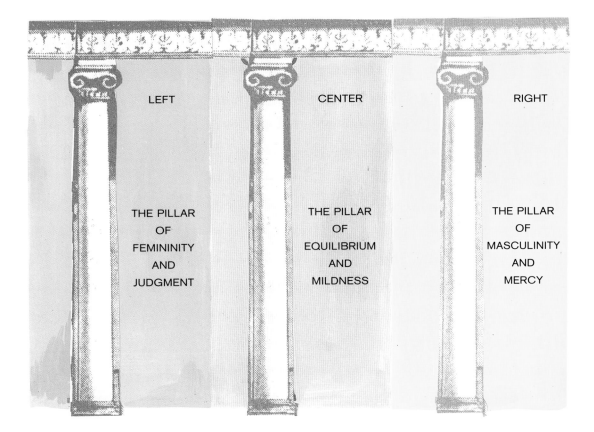

LEFT	CENTER	RIGHT
THE PILLAR OF FEMININITY AND JUDGMENT	THE PILLAR OF EQUILIBRIUM AND MILDNESS	THE PILLAR OF MASCULINITY AND MERCY

negative, and passive aspects, and consists of the spheres of *Binah*, *Gevurah*, and *Hod*.

The right-hand column, also called the *Pillar of Mercy*, consists of the spheres of *Hokhmah*, *Hessed*, and *Netzah*. This column is also described as having the principles of masculinity, activity, and positivity.

The central column, which is the balancing axis of the whole tree, is also known as the *Pillar of Mildness*, and consists of *Keter*, *Daat*, *Tiferet*, *Yesod*, and *Malkhut*.

The most common names and descriptions of the ten Sephirot are described as follows:

Above: *The qualities of the Sephirot can be expressed as three pillars (see p.130).*

KETER	Crown
HOKHMAH	Wisdom
BINAH	Understanding
HESSED	Love
GEVURAH	Severity
TIFERET	Beauty or harmony
NETZAH	Victory or endurance
HOD	Splendor or glory
YESOD	Foundation
MALKHUT	Sovereignty (this is often replaced by Shekhinah)

THE TREE OF LIFE AND THE SEPHIROT

KEY TO THE SEPHIROT

1 KETER (crown) **2** HOKHMAH (wisdom) **3** BINAH (understanding) **4** HESED (mercy)
5 GEVURAH (judgment) **6** TIFERET (beauty) **7** NETZAH (eternity) **8** HOD (glory) **9** YESOD
(foundation) **10** MALKHUT (kingdom)

THE TREE OF LIFE

THE MOST IMPORTANT symbol in Kabbalah is the Tree of Life. This is a diagram that represents the totality of creation—all that is, was, and will ever be. On one level it is a microcosmic key to creation, while on another level it can be used as a tool through which we can understand any event or circumstance.

The Tree of Life represents the whole of existence, and thus the energies and properties of each of the Sephirot can be seen to represent the whole of human knowledge. While their primary description is as Attributes of God, it is possible to define them in terms of human experience because we are cast in the image of God.

The diagram of the Tree of Life has developed through many stages of design before arriving at the modern three-columned form with which we are familiar today. It is from *Sepher Yetzirah* that we get the twenty-two pathways that are formulated on the twenty-two letters of the Hebrew alphabet upon which the creation of the universe is based.

The Sephirot which emanate from the AIN SOPH AUR are numbered ten because Kabbalists agree that ten is a perfect number, and because, in the original Hebrew, it contains every digit without repetition it is therefore the total essence of all numbers.

Above left: *The Hebrew letter Hei, which relates to the breath, and Daled (above right), which represents the Four Worlds (see pp. 27, 28).*

AIN SOPH AUR

THE DIVINE ENERGY OF THE CREATOR

Above: *Ancient Aramaic (pre-Hebrew) texts show inscriptions on the hands, symbols of healing.*

Situated between Binah and Hessed is a state of being known as Daat—knowledge—which, although it is not a Sephirah, acts and is often treated as one.

In order to comprehend the mental journey through the Four Worlds and the Sephirot of the Tree of Life, it is important to understand the multileveled symbolism. The *Zohar* contains detailed descriptions for each of the Sephirot to facilitate meditation, which includes their location in the Four Worlds and their corresponding divine emanation, human mental function, human body part, and Sacred Name. The following information on pages 33–38 is a brief illustration of some of the attributes of each of the Sephirot. The first path is Keter; the second is Hokhmah; the third, Binah; the center is Daat; the fourth path is Hessed; the fifth is Gevurah; the sixth path is Tiferet; the seventh is Netzah; the eighth is Hod; the ninth is Yesod; and the tenth is Malkhut/Shekhinah.

KETER

The first path is called Mystical Consciousness. It is the light which imparts understanding of the Beginning which has no beginning. No created being can attain to its essence.

SEPHER YETZIRAH

TRANSLATION:	Supreme crown.
LOCATION:	Top center.
DESCRIPTION:	Keter is the uppermost aspect of the Sephirot that can be contemplated by humans.
ARCHETYPAL WORLD:	Atzilut/Emanation.
HUMAN FUNCTION:	Will and humility.
BODY PART:	Crown and skull.
NAMES OF GOD:	EHYEH—I AM; the point of the tip of the letter *Yod* in the Tetragrammaton (the four-letter name of God).
OTHER SYMBOLS AND IMAGES:	Primordial ether; nothingness; the Ancient Holy One; before; the origin of will.

Above: *Keter means "supreme crown".*

HOKHMAH

The second path is called the Illuminating Intelligence. It is the Crown of Creation and the splendor of the Supreme Unity to which it is most in proximity. The Kabbalists call it the Second Splendor.

SEPHER YETZIRAH

Below: *Hokhmah, or "wisdom", signified by the oak.*

TRANSLATION:	Wisdom.
LOCATION:	Right side.
DESCRIPTION:	Hokhmah represents the contemplative aspects of God's thoughts. This is the primordial point of creation, the source of all wisdom and knowable reality.
ARCHETYPAL WORLD:	Atzilut/Emanation.
HUMAN FUNCTION:	Wisdom.
BODY PART:	Left ear, left lobe of brain.
NAMES OF GOD:	YAH; the letter *Yod* in the Tetragrammaton (the four-letter name of God).
OTHER SYMBOLS AND IMAGES:	Beginning; Eden; the origin of thought.
BIBLICAL FIGURE:	King Solomon.

Above: Binah is associated with understanding, symbolized by the hands.

Below right: Daat relates to wisdom and the center.

BINAH	

The third path is called the Sanctifying Intelligence. It is the foundation of Primordial Wisdom, termed the Creation of Faith. Its roots are AMeN. It is the Mother of Faith, which originates from it.

SEPHER YETZIRAH

TRANSLATION:	Discernment, understanding.
LOCATION:	Left side.
DESCRIPTION:	The analytical distinguishing aspects of God's thoughts.
ARCHETYPAL WORLD:	Atzilut/Emanation.
HUMAN FUNCTION:	Understanding.
BODY PART:	Right ear, right lobe of brain.
NAMES OF GOD:	YHVH ELOHIM (the Tetragrammaton as vocalized in the word *Elohim*—God.
OTHER SYMBOLS:	Supernal mother; supernal Shekhinah; womb; palace; repentance.
BIBLICAL FIGURE:	Leah.

DAAT

TRANSLATION:	Wisdom.
LOCATION:	Center.
DESCRIPTION:	The hidden Sephirah. There are no manifest correspondences because Daat represents direct meditation on AIN—nothingness.
ARCHETYPAL WORLD:	Atzilut/Emanation.
BODY PART:	Rear lobe of brain, throat, thyroid.
NAMES OF GOD:	YHVH ELOHIM.

HESSED

The fourth path is called the Receiving Intelligence because it arises like a boundary to receive the emanations of the higher intelligences which are sent down to it. Each emanates from the next by the power of Keter, the primordial emanation.

Sepher Yetzirah

Translation:	Love, compassion, greatness, loving kindness.
Location:	Right side.
Description:	The benevolent (masculine) side of God.
Archetypal world:	Beriya/Creation.
Human function:	Loving kindness, compassion.
Body part:	Left arm, left adrenal glands.
Names of God:	EL; Supreme God.
Other symbols and images:	Lion; upper waters.

Above: *Hessed means "love" and "compassion."*

GEVURAH

The fifth path is called the Radical Intelligence because it is more akin than any other to the Supreme Unity and emanates from the depths of the Primordial Wisdom (Hokhmah).

Sepher Yetzirah

Above: *Gevurah is associated with justice, law, and order.*

Translation:	Judgment, power.
Location:	Left side.
Description:	This Sephirah represents the powers of divine punishment and displeasure in the world. The power and divine energy needed to control the universe. It must also be understood that the destructive energy necessary to keep order and impose punishment also contains the seeds of demonic evil—the "other side."
Archetypal world:	Beriya/Creation.
Human function:	Strength.
Body part:	Right arm, right adrenal glands.
Name of God:	ELOHIM GIBOR.
Other symbols and images:	The Heavenly Court; north; fear (of Isaac, see Genesis 31:53); gold; great and consuming fire; the severe attribute of justice; bread; wine; salt; meat.
Biblical figure:	Isaac.

TIFERET

The sixth path is called the Inflowing Intuitive Consciousness because the flux of emanations is multiplied therein. It transmits this influence to those blessed men who are united with it.

SEPHER YETZIRAH

Above: *Tiferet, like the bird, is a mystic symbol of the spirit and intuition.*

TRANSLATION: Beauty, glory

LOCATION: Center.

DESCRIPTION: The perfect balance between justice and mercy needed for the efficient and loving control of the universe. This Sephirah unites all of the nine upper powers. It contains the combined energies of Hohkmah (wisdom) and Binah (understanding).

ARCHETYPAL WORLD: Beriya/Creation.

HUMAN FUNCTION: Self-consciousness.

BODY PART: Heart, spine, torso, blood, veins, arteries.

NAMES OF GOD: The Tetragrammaton (YHVH—the four-lettered name of God); the letter *Vav* of the Tetragrammaton; YHVH Eloah Ve-Daat; the Holy One, Blessed be He (the common epithet in Rabbinical literature for God).

OTHER SYMBOLS AND IMAGES: Compassion, truth.

BIBLICAL FIGURES: Jacob, Moses, Adam.

NETZAH

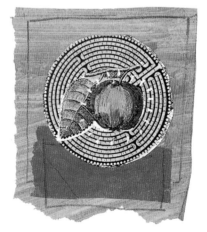

Above: *The goodness of Netzah is hidden within the universal maze.*

The seventh path is called the Hidden Intelligence because it puts out a brilliant splendor on all intellectual virtues which are seen with the eyes of the spirit and by the ecstasy of faith.

SEPHER YETZIRAH

TRANSLATION: Splendor, eternity, endurance, victory.

LOCATION: Right side.

DESCRIPTION: The active goodness of God's presence in this world.

ARCHETYPAL WORLD: Yetzira/Formation.

HUMAN FUNCTION: Determination.

BODY PART: Left leg, left kidney.

NAME OF GOD: YHVH ZEVA'OT (Lord of Hosts).

OTHER SYMBOLS AND IMAGES: The right pillar (Jachin) in the Temple (1 Kings 7:21).

BIBLICAL FIGURE: Moses.

HOD

The eighth path is called Perfect and Absolute Intelligence. From it emanates the organizing principles. Its roots are in the depths of the Sphere Magnificence, from the very substance of which it emanates.

Sepher Yetzirah

TRANSLATION:	Majesty.
LOCATION:	Left side.
DESCRIPTION:	Hod represents the lower channel through which the judgment of God is brought upon the world.
ARCHETYPAL WORLD:	Yetzira/Formation.
HUMAN FUNCTION:	Flexibility.
BODY PART:	Right leg, right kidney.
NAME OF GOD:	ELOHIM ZEVA'OT (God of Hosts).
OTHER SYMBOLS AND IMAGES:	The left pillar (Boaz) in the Temple (1 Kings 7:21).
BIBLICAL FIGURE:	Aaron.

Above: *Hod represents the majestic rays of God's judgment.*

YESOD

The ninth path is called Pure Intelligence. It purifies the Sephirot, proves and corrects their design. It establishes their unity, so that they may not be destroyed or divided.

Sepher Yetzirah

Below: *Yesod is the path of pure intelligence.*

TRANSLATION:	Foundation.
LOCATION:	Center.
DESCRIPTION:	This is the channel through which Tiferet strives to unite with the Shekhinah—the presence of God.
ARCHETYPAL WORLD:	Yetzira/Formation.
HUMAN FUNCTION:	Spiritual aspiration.
BODY PART:	Genitals.
NAMES OF GOD:	ELOHIM HAYYIM (the living God); SHADDAI EL HAI (God Almighty).
OTHER SYMBOLS AND IMAGES:	The Tree of Life; source of living waters; rainbow; remembrance; the righteous one; oath; lover; redeemer.
BIBLICAL FIGURE:	Joseph.

MALKHUT/SHEKHINAH

The tenth path is called the Resplendent Intelligence, because it is exalted above every head and has its seat in Understanding (Binah). It enlightens the fire of all lights and emanates the power of the principal forms.

SEPHER YETZIRAH

Above: *Malkhut relates to the presence of God and the feminine aspect of creation.*

TRANSLATION: God's presence, kingdom.

LOCATION: Center.

DESCRIPTION: The Shekinah is a Talmudic concept illustrating God's presence in the created world. It is through the Shekhinah that we can experience the Divine and receive the energy of the higher Sephirot. The compassion and passivity of the Shekhinah is often equated with its femininity.

ARCHETYPAL WORLD: Assiya/Action.

HUMAN FUNCTION: Perception.

BODY PART: Mouth, feet, skeleton.

NAMES OF GOD: ADONAI HA-ARETZ (Lord of the Earth); the last letter in the Tetragrammaton (the four-letter name of God.

OTHER SYMBOLS AND IMAGES: The Shekhinah is often displayed as a bride or princess whose male lover is the composite of the nine upper Sephirot, represented by the prince/bridegroom.

BIBLICAL FIGURES: King David, Rachel.

The Connecting Pathways

Below: *Gimel reflects the quality of kindness.*

THE SEPHIROT ARE interconnected by twenty-two pathways. They represent the energies which flow between the Sephirot, eventually aspiring to reach the divine source of the Creator.

The Hebrew word for "paths" is *nativot*, meaning hidden or undiscovered paths. These paths can only be accessed by states of consciousness accomplished by particular spiritual realizations. They can only be accessed by the individual soul in its journey to understanding cosmic manifestation and spiritual awareness. The rest areas dotted along the route that this journey takes are the Sephirot, and the different routes that lead there are the paths, each with its unique energy.

Each of the connecting pathways are linked with colors, Hebrew letters, archetypal images, healing energies, an element, planet, or Zodiac sign. Their Tarot correspondences are illustrated in Chapters 2, 4, and 5.

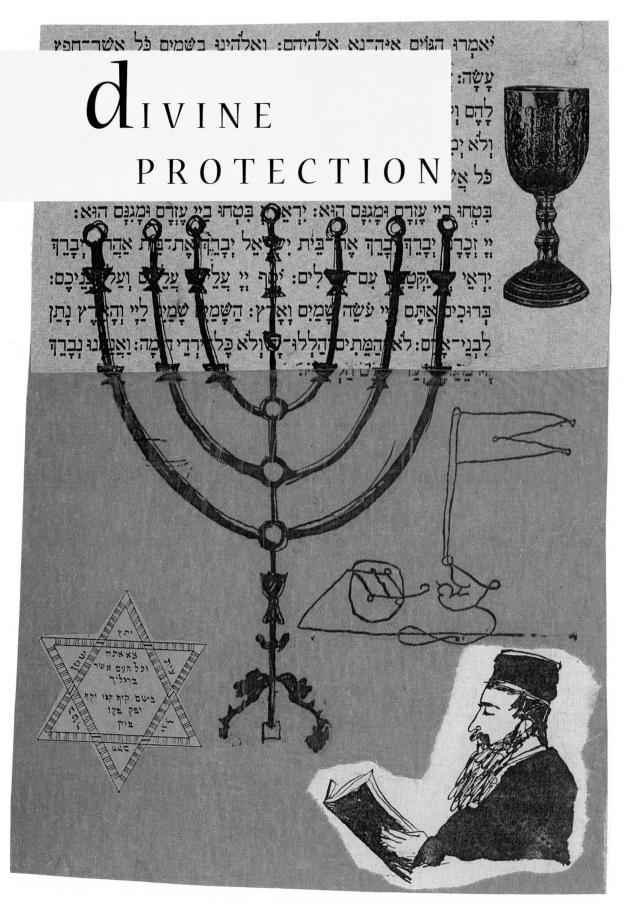

dIVINE PROTECTION

dIVINE PROTECTION

ALTHOUGH KABBALAH TEACHES us about spirituality and goodness, it also recognizes that there is great evil all around us, which can not only lead us astray, but can also physically harm us. The spiritual world abounds with witches, demons, and dybbuks who are out to cause us mischief, and we are also at the mercy of the people all around us, who may, consciously or unconsciously, wish us harm.

Below: *Beit (top) relates to peace, and Aleph (bottom) to creativity.*

WHEN WE THINK OF evil, we often think of the devil or Satan versus the good of God. Kabbalah teaches us that there is only one God, and that the evil figure depicted as the Devil or Satan is in fact His agent, who is sent to test the will of man. This war of attrition of good versus evil, which has been played since the beginning of time, really consists of the so-called Devil tempting us to be evil, when in fact he is actually working for God—a bit of a "sting" operation really! This is illustrated in the beginning of the Book of Job, when it is clear that Satan is actually a member of the Court of Heaven who is then sent out to test Job's righteousness. In fact, it is God who lays down the ground rules that Job himself must not be touched (Job 1:6–12).

In other words, the Devil/Satan who seeks to lead us astray is actually an agent of God, who is always testing our inner worthiness. It is only when we consider the force of evil as being apart from God that we can be harmed by it. Through Kabbalah we learn to recognize that evil is in fact a creation of God, as is stated in Isaiah 45:7: "I form light and create darkness. I make peace and create evil: I am the Lord, I do all these things."

The purpose of evil is to present us all with a free choice of which pathway we wish to tread. Without the presence of evil, we would have no alternative but to always be good and pure, and thus there would be no virtue in the good that we do. However, God has given us free will to be able

to choose which path we wish to follow, and the presence of evil is an important ingredient in His plan.

We are all open to this evil temptation, and it is always present, causing us to show our weaknesses and uncertainties. Have you not heard that tiny whisper inside your head that arouses feelings of jealousy, anger, envy, ruthlessness, and vindictiveness, just to mention a few negative thoughts? It is the same voice that gives rise to feelings of hopelessness, fear, anxiety, worry, and depression.

Therefore we see that we live in a world where good does fight evil through us. This has led man to develop ways of "white magic," which can be used either when we give in to the temptations of Satan—through our own thoughts and actions, or through the thoughts and actions of others—to help us achieve divine protection from all forms of evil.

Many writings in Kabbalah mention various types of good/white magic and ways in which we can seek divine protection, such as blessings, prayers, and amulets. Most of the written and oral Kabbalah has been primarily taught by generations of rabbis—an elite male group. Within this there are many, many references to the supernatural. However, even more important to us in looking at the Kabbalist world of superstition and protection, is the grassroots tradition that has mainly been passed down orally through innumerable generations of women.

Above: *In Kaballah, good and evil can be perceived as an internal battle between positive and negative thoughts.*

41

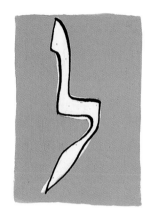

FOOLING THE EVIL SPIRIT

Above: *The letter Lamed (top) stands for righteousness, and Kaph (bottom) for intention and will.*

What's in a Name?

THE GIVEN NAME of a person is very important in Kabbalah, and this can be seen to be carried through to other beliefs. In order that the Angel of Death does not make a mistake and take the wrong life, children are not named after living relatives. It is also believed by many Ashkenazi (Eastern European) Jews that to name a child after a living relative could cause the soul of that relative to become weak, because the name and the soul are very closely linked. In Poland, when several people in a family had recently died, a newborn was given a name that was never spoken, so as to give the evil spirits no opportunity. Sometimes a nickname, such Alte (old one), was given to a child in order to deceive the Angel of Death.

All Jewish babies are given a Hebrew name, which is one of the most important decisions the parents make. Because the Talmud teaches that this Hebrew name will have an influence on the life and character of the child, it is important that the individual from whom this name derives has led a good and fortunate life.

Isaac Luria, the legendary Kabbalist, wrote that the good or bad behavior and nature of a person can be discovered by analyzing this name. It could be, for example, a biblical name such as my father's, whose middle name was Abraham, or it could be Sarah or Rachel for a girl. It is often said that parents are actually predicting the future when naming their newborn, because they are naming them with names that will fittingly describe their personalities and destinies.

According to the Arizel, the numerical value of the Hebrew letters in one's name is another extremely important factor on the life that person is going to live (see Gemetria on page 148). This also can apply to any nickname given to a person.

Rabbi Elimelech of Lyzhansk, one of the founders of Hassidism in Galicia, Poland, wrote that there is a strong connection between the soul of a child and the soul of the person for whom they were named. When a baby is named after a departed soul, the latter's soul is elevated to a higher realm

Above: *The Hebrew letter Yod brings energy and change.*

in Heaven, and a spiritual affinity is created between the soul of the departed and the soul of the newborn. This spiritual bond can have a profound impact on the child. For example, the Hebrew word for soul— *neshma*—is spelled with the four Hebrew letters Nun, Shin, Mem, and Hei. The Hebrew word for name, *shem*—spelled Shin, Mem—is contained within the word *neshma*, showing the strong connection between one's name and one's soul.

It is precisely due to the combinations of fortune and misfortune of the soul after which the child is named, together with the concealed secrets of the numerology in that given name, that when a person is seriously ill they will be given an additional name such as Chaim, meaning "life," or a whole new name in order to influence the destiny of their soul. We hope and pray that the new name will herald a new phase of *mazel*—luck—for the unfortunate person.

YOUR NAME AND YOUR SOUL

Hei   *Mem*   *Shin*   *Nun*

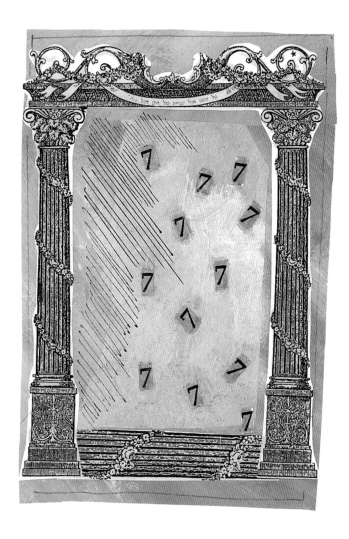

Mirror, Mirror on the Wall

THE USE OF MIRRORS includes some of the oldest superstitions and rituals that are still practiced today. A mirror is thought to reflect another version of the original, and if a mirror is damaged it is believed that we are damaging ourselves. Therefore it can be said that damaging our reflection is damaging our soul. The saying "seven years' bad luck" stems from the belief that the body changes its physiological make-up every seven years, and any disturbance in a reflection can cause a deterioration between the body and soul.

If you do break or damage a mirror, do not despair, because there are remedies that will lead to your soul's damage limitation. You could neutralize any potential evil by either washing the broken pieces in a south-running river, or by burying them in the ground. Whatever you do, do not look into the broken mirror, and remove it from your home.

When a Jewish person dies, after the burial the family usually sits *shiva* (mourning) for seven days. All the mirrors in the home are covered during this period so that the departing soul cannot be tempted to take the soul of a living relative along for company. This is standard practice in most Jewish homes, even today.

DYBBUKS AND DEMONS

Dybbuks

THE HEBREW WORD *dybbuk* comes from a word meaning "clinging" or "cleaving." A dybbuk is a wandering, disembodied soul which is not at rest and looks for an already occupied body that is left vulnerable for a number of reasons, into which it enters and holds fast. The dybbuk speaks through the occupied person's mouth with a new voice, and a change of personality takes place. Sometimes a dybbuk is not a human soul but a demon who attaches itself to a woman, who it may try to turn into a witch.

A dybbuk is usually driven out by an exorcism being performed, and leaves the inhabited body through the little toe. Before it can be removed it must be made to identify itself, so that the Rabbi can say the correct prayers that allow the soul to be laid to rest. If it is removed without this process, it will try to find another body to attach itself to.

Belief in such spirits was common in the sixteenth and seventeenth centuries in Eastern Europe, and individuals who were probably suffering from nervous or mental disorders were often taken to rabbis, who would perform an exorcism.

Chaim Vital Calabrese (1543–1620), a leading disciple of Isaac Luria, told of a man who fathered a number of illegitimate children while committing adultery. When he died, his soul wandered for twenty-five years until it was able to possess a woman while she was angry. It was able to enter her house because there was no mezuzah on the door.

There are many stories in Kabbalah about people being possessed by dybbuks. There is also the famous play *The Dybbuk*, which was written in around 1916 by the Jewish scholar and folklorist S. Ansky; it was originally in Yiddish, and has since been translated and played in many languages around the world. This story is set at the end of the nineteenth century and

Left: *The Hebrew letter Tzaddi (top) means "righteous"; and Pei (bottom), is associated with communication.*

tells of two ill-fated lovers—Chanon, a devout but penniless student of the Kabbalah, and Leah, the young woman whom he adores. Unknown to them, they had been betrothed since birth, but Leah's father breaks the marriage contract by offering Leah to a rich man.

Chanon, who is weak from prolonged fasting and prayer, dies instantly on hearing the news and becomes a dybbuk, who enters Leah's body, attempting to possess her love for eternity. Most of the play is centered around the Kabbalistic attempts to exorcize the dybbuk from Leah. In the end, rather than face a marriage to a man she does not love, Leah chooses an unworldly union with the tormented spirit of Chanon.

Demons

Demons were created at twilight on the eve of the first Sabbath.

BASED ON *ETHICS OF THE FATHERS*, 5:6

Let the earth bring forth living creatures.

GENESIS 1:25

THESE "LIVING CREATURES," according to Rabbi Judah 1, the Patriarch, were the demons. The Holy One created their souls, but when He was about to create their bodies the Sabbath's sanctity began, and He would not create them.

Because demons were made in the split second just before the first Sabbath of creation, God did not have time to give them bodies, so they remained disembodied spirits.

The fear of demons and evil spirits took hold in Medieval times, evolving from established Talmudic and Kabbalist writings. Demons were described as being between angels and men, and their attributes included invisibility, wings, and being unable to cast shadows. They usually lived in uninhabited places, and could disguise themselves as humans, animals, or even inanimate objects.

One of the main early influences was inherited from the Babylonian Jews, who had lived in exile in a world inhabited with spirits and demons, some benevolent, and others malevolent. They were invisible:

"If the eye could see them, no one could endure them. They surround one on all sides. They are more numerous then humans, each person has a thousand on his left and then a thousand on his right."

The presence and location of demons was very specific. They inhabited the air and the trees; water, the roofs of houses, and privies (bathrooms). Night-time was thought to be an especially dangerous time, particularly for those who slept alone, or did things in pairs (therefore including the majority of the population). At particular times it was considered dangerous to drink water, because the menstrual blood of demonesses was said to poison certain wells.

Kabbalah attempts to systematize demonology, although the cultural environment and outlook of each individual Kabbalist has contributed towards a diverse spread of beliefs.

Nahmanides wrote that demons (*shedim*) are to be found in waste (*shedudim*), ruined, cold, and uninhabited places. He concluded that they are created out of fire and air. Their subtle bodies are invisible to humans, and they can fly through fire and air. In the *Midrash* we learn that semen that has been wastefully discharged can be used by evil spirits to produce their own kind.

In the *Talmud* we learn to fear the night, because this is when the demons come out:

"It is forbidden to greet one another by night, for we fear that the other might be a demon." (Megilla 3a)

Above and below: *Some Kabbalists believe that demons are created by fire and air, and that they inhabit water.*

Above: *As a demonic lair, a pond, drunk from at night was thought to be highly dangerous.*

Demons are usually harmful, and can cause disease. This is demonstrated in the following passage, and we also are given the antidote for this danger, which resembles an "abracadabra" amulet, where each succeeding line is reduced by one letter (see page 61):

> Our rabbis taught: A person should not drink water from rivers or pools at night, and if one drinks, his blood is on his own head because of the danger. What is the danger? The danger of the "shabriri" [demon of blindness]. But if he is thirsty, what is the remedy? If a person is with him, he should say to him, "So-and-so, the son of so-and-so, I am thirsty for water." But if not, let him say to himself,
> "O so-and-so, my mother told me,
> 'Beware of the
> **SHABRIRI**
> **BRIRI**
> **RIRI**
> **IRI**
> **RI**
> **R'**
> I am thirsty for water in a white glass."
>
> TALMUD, PESACHIM 112A

THE *ZOHAR* TRACES the origin of demons to the results of sexual intercourse between humans and demonic powers, while later Kabbalist writings talk about demons who are born to humans, thus creating illegitimate offspring called *banim shovavim* (mischievous sons). When death arrives, these sons accompany the dead person and stake a claim on the dead person's estate. This is the reason for the custom of circling the dead in a cemetery in order to repulse the demons.

There are many times when we are particularly susceptible to demons and dybbuks causing havoc with our physical bodies, and it is when we are at our weakest that we must fool them.

The *Zohar* teaches that the spirits of evil men become demons after their death, but it also teaches that there are good-natured demons who are prepared to do favors and help mankind. It mentions that those demons ruled by Ashmedal (Asmodeus), who accepted the Torah, are considered "Jewish demons."

It is also written in the *Zohar* that demons often make fun of men, and tell them lies about the future, and invade their dreams, mixing the truth with lies. Their feet are described as being crooked (*Zohar* 3:229b), and in various Kabbalist sources four mothers of demons are mentioned: Lilith, Naaman, Agrah, and Mahalath (sometimes replaced by Rahab).

At appointed times the demons who are ruled by these "mothers" go out into the world and cause danger and carnage. At specific times and places they teach male and female witches the art of the occult and witchcraft.

Above: *The Hebrew letters Ayin (top) and Samekh (below), respectively represent intuition and the protection of God.*

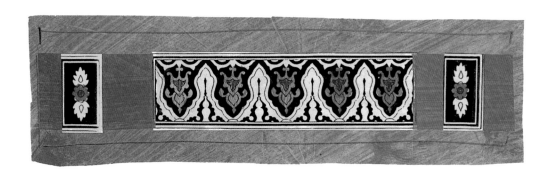

Above: *The Hebrew letter Nun is symbolic of the cycles of life.*

LILITH

The wild creatures of the desert shall meet with the jackals. The goat demon shall call to his fellow, the lilith shall also repose there and find for herself a place of rest.

Isaiah 34:14

Without doubt Lilith is the most famous demon, and dozens of conflicting stories and traditions abound about her. We first find mention of her in a work called the *Alphabet of Ben-Sira*, which was probably written about 600–1000 CE, although many scholars believe that the Lilith legend and traditions could be much older. This story seems to merge into two separate traditions—that of the Lilith of the *Talmud*, and that which portrays Lilith as the "first Eve."

LILITH IN THE *TALMUD*

In the Babylonian *Talmud*, Lilith is described as a wild-haired and winged female demon with a woman's face (Eruvin 100b). She seems to have nymphomaniac tendencies, as, according to Rabbi Haninah (Shabbat 151b), any person sleeping alone in a house is liable to be seized by her. She is also the mother of demons, and we are told that the demon Hormin is one of her sons (Batra 73a).

LILITH IN THE *MIDRASH*—THE "FIRST EVE"

Adam and Lilith began to fight. She said, "I will not lie below," and he said, "I will not lay beneath you, but only on top. For you are fit only to be in the bottom position, while I am to be in the superior one."

ALPHABET OF BEN-SIRA

Right: *Tav is a symbol of spiritual learning.*
Left: *Mem is the first letter of the Hebrew word molech, or angel.*

THE *ALPHABET OF BEN-SIRA* tells us how God created a woman out of the earth as a companion for Adam. This woman was called Lilith. She demanded equality with Adam, and took offence that when they were having sex she was forced into the recumbent position. As a result they quarrelled, and when Adam tried to compel her obedience by force, she grew angry and flew through the air to the Red Sea.

God sent three angels—Sanvai, Sansanvai, and Semanglof—in an unsuccessful attempt to bring Lilith back. God warned that if she refused to return, then one hundred of her children would die every day. The angels found Lilith at the Red Sea and told her God's warning, but she refused to return. When told of her punishment, she vowed to inflict harm on all male infants up to the eighth day after their birth, and on females up to the twentieth day after their birth. She swore to the angels that whenever she saw their names or forms on an amulet, she would not harm the infant. She also agreed to have one hundred of her children die every day. It is therefore taught that every day one hundred demons perish.

LILITH IN KABBALAH

THERE ARE VARIOUS and often contradictory accounts found in Kabbalistic texts of different periods, but on the whole Lilith's image is depicted as complex and evil. While some relate to the myth as laid out in the account in the *Alphabet of Ben-Sira*, the *Zohar* theorizes that Adam was originally a hermaphrodite constituting both the male and female elements. This is then further elaborated by the writer Rabbi Levi, who says:

When man was created, he was created with two body fronts, and He sawed him in two, so that two bodies resulted, one for the male and one for the female.

Left: *Lilith is often represented as a demonized femme fatale, symbolized in Western culture by the mermaid. Some Kabbalist texts see her as a taker of newborn babies, against whom amulets are the only protection.*

Below: *The letter Shin.*

The *Zohar*, expanding on the theme of Adam's hermaphroditic nature, then relates it to Lilith:

> **"The female was attached to the side of the male until God cast him into a deep slumber... God then sawed her off from him and adorned her like a bride and brought her to him, as it is written, and He took one of his sides and closed up the place with flesh."**

The interesting point about both this quote and the text in the *Alphabet* is that Lilith is seen as being totally equal to Adam, either being created from the same earth, or from being half of the original hermaphrodite. However, her feminist and free-spirited attitude is totally out of being with later Kabbalist texts, and her equality with Adam is no longer allowed for, as can been seen from a commentary on Genesis 2:23. The biblical text states:

Now this, at last—bone from my bones, flesh from my flesh!—this shall be called woman.

The writer of the seventeenth-century book of Kabbalistic legends called the *Yalhut Re'uvenie* comments on the above by saying:

In the beginning when the Holy One, blessed be He, created (the first) Eve, he did not create her out of flesh, but rather of the filth of the earth and the sediment.

In the same book, we find the claim that Lilith, together with another female demon called Naamah, had intercourse with Adam and brought forth "plagues to the world."

In the mystical tradition taught in Kabbalah, Lilith seems to have two primary functions. She seduces men, and through their nocturnal emissions gives birth to hundreds of demonic children. On the other hand, all newborn infants are at her mercy, unless they are protected from her by the use of amulets. She is also periodically described in Kabbalah as a seducer of men and a demonic witch.

Protecting Your Children

AMULETS CONTAINING THE NAMES of the three angels, Sanvai, Sansanvai, and Semanglof, will protect the newborn infant against Lilith, because she promised God that she will not kill any newborn who is protected by these names. Similar amulets will protect women giving birth, and should be placed over the bed and on all four walls of the room.

Boys are susceptible until they are circumcised, usually any time after the eighth day after their birth. Girls must be protected by amulets for up to twenty days after their birth.

Above and above right:

A knife under the pillow of women in labor protects against demons, and red ribbon and garlic near a baby's cot guard against Lilith.

A sharp metal knife is placed under the pillow of women giving birth, because demons do not like metal. In some communities, candy is placed under the bed of the mother during labor, in order to distract the attention of the evil spirits away from her and the baby.

Sometimes, when a baby laughs in its sleep it could be that Lilith is playing with it. It is therefore advisable to tap the baby on its nose to shoo Lilith away. Red ribbon and garlic should be placed on or near a baby's cot. My mother always made sure that I had some red ribbon either sewn on to the baby's undergarments, or attached with a diaper pin when my children were babies.

The colors red and blue help protect against demons, and spitting three times in their direction will push away evil spirits.

Demons, Evil Spirits, and Weddings

A BRIDE AND GROOM are particularly susceptible during and just after their wedding, because it is believed that demons and evil spirits are extremely jealous of the bridegroom.

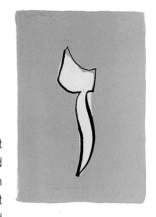

In order to fool the demons, who can be particularly stupid, ash is put onto the faces of the bride and groom so that they do not look beautiful and radiant. In some Hassidic communities even today, the bride and groom enter the synagogue crying and praying, because they are taught that at this spiritual period in their lives they are very close to God, and they should pray for their community. In fact, the origins of this practice are often forgotten, but because a bride and groom are normally radiant and happy, this act of penance for the community puts the demons totally off-track.

In the same way, the bride and groom are often guarded on their wedding night. In some communities, the new bride and groom do not leave their new home for seven days, until the danger of being susceptible to demons passes. The bridegroom should not be left alone on his wedding day, because he will be susceptible to demons and the evil eye.

In some Sephardic (Middle Eastern) communities, the bride messes up her hair after the ceremony, again to fool the demons into believing that she is not happy and radiant. In some Jewish weddings, two candles are carried to escort the bride and bridegroom to the *chuppah* (wedding canopy) because demons are frightened by fire and light.

At the end of every Jewish marriage ceremony today, a glass is broken. Many people believe that this custom stems from the destruction of the two Temples in

Above: *The letter Vav.*
Below left: *The letter Hei.*

Below: *A glass is broken at the end of Jewish weddings to protect against evil.*

Above: *Daled (top) teaches us to develop our sixth sense. Gimel (bottom) encourages growth and generosity.*

Jerusalem, but in fact the noise from the glass breaking is a protective measure against demons, evil spirits, and ill-wishers. During the Middle Ages in Germany, there was a special stone, called a *traustein*, embedded in the outside north wall of a synagogue for the glass to be smashed against. The splinters of glass were thought to hit demons who descended from the north, and would protect against their evil.

During the marriage ceremony, the bridegroom is in mortal danger from demons and evil spirits until the bride walks either three times or seven times around him under the bridal canopy. An important aspect of this is that she is also making a protective circle around the bridegroom—hence a "magic circle."

Demons, Evil Spirits, and Death

PREGNANT WOMEN SHOULD NOT go to burial grounds, because they are particularly susceptible to evil spirits and dybbuks entering them. Your hands must always be washed under running water when leaving burial grounds, in order to prevent any evil spirits from possibly clinging to them and leaving with you.

I was brought up in the tradition that I must not go to the burial grounds while both my parents were alive, because this would be asking for evil to befall them. When leaving a cemetery, some people pluck some blades of grass and throw them behind their backs in order to repel any evil spirits that may be lurking.

The household water should be poured out if there has been a death, so that evil spirits and demons cannot cross over the water. This also prevents the soul from being trapped inside the house.

A deceased corpse should not be left alone before burial, and family or members of the community sit and watch, reading the Psalms, just in case the evil spirits try to carry off the corpse.

THE EVIL EYE

SUPERSTITIONS INVOLVING the evil eye have permeated into every culture and civilization throughout history. Although some of you may laugh when you read this, how many of you have felt bad vibes about someone, or have felt mentally and emotionally drained after speaking to someone, either in person or by telephone? I have had enough people come to me to ask me for help to know that this problem still exists today, although under a different guise—bad vibes, emotionally draining, energy vampires, and being under psychic attack, are just some of the descriptions of how people can feel about others in their environment.

In Kabbalah, the evil eye stems from two sources. Either it is from someone who is jealous and spiteful, or it can originate from an independent malevolent force that prowls the world and is associated with demons. This force generates from a bad angel who is called into being by an evil glance or thought.

Hidden away in the mystical practices of Kabbalah there are little-known ways in which you can not only protect yourself, but you can also clear away these bad vibes, and in one of the rituals that I am going to describe they can actually be sent back to where they came from.

I was taught by my father that the power of the mind is so strong that not only can people consciously wish evil upon others, but sometimes this can also subconsciously happen, for example when people are jealous of you— perhaps you have just got engaged, got that promotion, or had praise from your boss?

The measures taken to avoid the evil eye take two forms: preventative and counteractive.

Above: *The letter Aleph (right) represents strength. Beit (left) relates to peacefulness.*

KENANAH HORA

MAY THERE BE NO EVIL EYE

Above: *The letter Lamed is associated with justice.*

Below: *The Chai amulet.*

Preventative Measures Against the Evil Eye

FROM EARLY CHILDHOOD, I was taught in the more mystical aspects of Kabbalah that there are many practical ways to prevent the evil eye from falling upon you:

Never brag about *anything*. This is asking for trouble, because it will lead to jealous thoughts being directed against you. In particular, never boast about any type of success, either personal or to do with your family, otherwise you will be leaving both yourself and your nearest and dearest open to bad vibes.

Babies are particularly susceptible to the evil eye, so never, ever praise any newborn who is related to you to others. Do not talk about your children in front of women who are childless. Put a piece of Passover matzo into the pocket of your children to protect them.

The breaking of glass at a wedding with help avert the evil eye from the happiness of the bride and groom. Avoid a double wedding in one household. In Turkey, it was traditional to sew or pin a blue bead beneath a bride's wedding gown to protect her from the evil eye.

If anyone praises you or your family, say the phrase *kaynayenahora* (may there be no evil eye), and also say *per, per, per* (as if spitting), so that if there is any jealous intent involved it will not be able to touch you or your family.

Amulets for Protection

AN AMULET IS A charm that is often inscribed with a symbol or magical incantation to protect the wearer against evil and will help bring good fortune. Amulets have been used in Kabbalah since Medieval times. Traditionally, they were made to order and would name the individual who they were to protect—if written on parchment, it was important that this was virgin material.

Amulets cover a wide spectrum of uses, from protecting against the evil eye and use in childbirth, to protecting from Lilith and against scorpions, as well as against illnesses and the plague. These pages show some examples of amulets that are still in common use today; most of the jewelry can be purchased in almost any shopping mall or main street.

The **CHAI** represents the blessing *le chai'im*—"to life." This amulet consists of the letters Chet and Yod which, combined, make up the numerical value of 18, a number that has been imbued with magical properties throughout history.

The **HAMSA** (an Arabic word meaning five) is in the shape of a hand. The Judaic tradition of using this as a protective amulet predates the Muslim use of the Hamsa (called the hand of Fatima, daughter of Mohammed) by at least a thousand years. The Hebrew name for this amulet is *hamash*, which comes from the Hebrew word for five. It symbolizes the protective hand of the Creator, and is often to be found decorated with an eye (the watchful eye of the Creator), and often the eye is blue, to ward off evil spirits.

The **STAR OF DAVID** is also referred to as the Seal of Solomon. This six-pointed star was mainly used in non-Jewish European magic to ward off evil and to master spirits. It began to be used in Kabbalistic amulets roughly around the twelfth century, and is also used to attract good luck, as well as protecting against misfortune caused by demons, evil spirits, and the evil eye. I usually wear this myself as an extra protection when healing. It is also often inscribed on the outside of the mezuzah.

The **MEZUZAH** is a small cylinder that is placed at the entrance to all Jewish homes, and often on the doorway to every room in the house except the bathroom. It serves to remind the occupants of the house of God, and protects all those who enter.

Above and below:

Inscriptions and motifs, such as the Star of David, form the basis of many protective amulets.

It contains two handwritten biblical passages, and must strictly conform to certain rules:

- **It must be written out perfectly, with no mistakes.**
- **It must be handwritten by a fully qualified scribe.**

- **It must contain the two biblical passages referred to, the Shema (Deuteronomy 6:4–9) and the Vehaya (Deuteronomy 11:13–21). Both passages contain the commandment "and thou shalt write them upon the door-posts of thy house and upon thy gates."**

When the Mezuzah is fitted, the following prayer from the *Siddur*—the daily prayer book—should be said:

We ask His blessing on this home and all who live in it. May its doors be opened up to those in need and its rooms be filled with kindness. May love dwell within its walls, and joy shine from its window. May His peace protect it and His presence never leave it.

THE SHEMA IS USUALLY then recited—the full copy of this prayer is available on page 107.

If the people in a house that is protected by the Mezuzah are undergoing bad times, Kabbalists will send someone over to inspect the Mezuzah to make sure that it is still "kosher," i.e. that it is in perfect condition, or to see if it needs replacing .

FISH AMULETS derive from both Kabbalist and Christian traditions, where the fish is a symbol of fertility and abundance; there is a prevalence of the fish symbol on many Kabbalistic manuscripts and amulets. Fish are popular

as amulets because they are seen to be so plenteous in the sea, therefore the wearing of this amulet will have an affect on fertility and abundance.

Many wedding manuscripts (*ketubbot*) include fish within the illustrations, and there is a variety of fish amulets for barren women: in Sephardic Jewish books of charms, there are many remedies, charms, and customs that encourage fish being eaten by women who have ceased to bear children. The fish is also a symbol to encourage male fertility, and because fish live under the sea they are considered immune to the evil eye.

The **MAGIC TRIANGLE**—by writing a magical word and then reducing the size of the inscription, the power of an evil spirit or demon is significantly diminished. The magical word "abracadabra," which is derived from Aramaic, is probably the most famous magical incantation in the world. Not only is it still widely used today, but in Medieval times many would wear the written formulae of this word in the following way, to ward off and protect against diseases:

Above: *The letter Tet (right), indicates divine goodness. Yod (center) symbolizes change, and Kaph (left) represents willpower and awareness.*

```
A B R A C A D A B R A
 A B R A C A D A B R
  A B R A C A D A B
   A B R A C A D A
    A B R A C A D
     A B R A C A
      A B R A C
       A B R A
        A B R
         A B
          A
```

SQUARES AND RECTANGLES—pieces of virgin parchment were divided into boxes, in which Hebrew letters were written. These were then folded up and secretly placed within an amulet. In some cases the power would be in the letters forming words, while in others it would be the power of the numerical value of the letters that would be the source of the amulet's power (see page 150).

Magical squares, or *kameas*, are an important aspect of talismanic magic. Kabbalah teaches that it is possible to demonstrate a graphic representation of any name on these squares by working out the numerical value of a name according to Gemetria (see page 148) and then tracing a line connecting these numbers of the kamea. This connecting line is called a *sigil* (this is a magic diagram that is composed of the essence of the name of either a spirit or person). Once the sigil of a name has been found, it can be used, either by itself or on the squares, for a variety of magical uses. These Kabbalist magic squares can contain anything from between nine to a hundred boxes, each containing a significant letter.

I recently found it fascinating when discussing Kabbalist amulets with my elderly mother, that she referred to all amulets such as the Chai or Star of David as kameas (pronounced as kamias) without knowing the meaning, and as far as she was concerned this had always been the case.

BABYLONIAN DEMON BOWLS are unique in their wide range of protective magic. Dating from between the third and first centuries BCE to the sixth century CE, they are only found in several sites in Iran and Iraq. Usually they are inscribed in one of three Aramaic dialects—Jewish-Aramaic, Syriac, and Mandaic—although a small number has been found inscribed in Persian (Pehlevi).

They usually consist of a terracotta bowl inscribed with magical text and charms, and were used to drive away evil. They would be inverted and buried under the four corners of the foundations of houses and buildings. The magic in the bowls was conceived mainly for two purposes: first as a protection against an assortment of evils, including illnesses, curses, demons, and the evil eye. Others have been found which, due to their

Above right: *The letter Chet.*

Below: *The letter Zayin.*

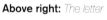

engraved images of bound demons and because they were in a space that also included human skull fragments and inscribed eggshells, were probably set as demon traps. They were meant to lure, trap, and disable any demons, thereby preventing them from hurting humans and causing damage to buildings.

Some bowls have also been found with inscriptions, leading to the belief that they were used to send the demons to do their evil on the person's enemy. These bowls would sometimes be buried in cemeteries where the demons and ghosts would ply their trade; others, which would perhaps work even more efficiently, would be buried next to the victim's house.

SALT has been used since ancient times for its protective properties. According to Kabbalists, salt must be set on a table before a meal begins, because "it protects one against Satan's denunciations." Kabbalah is very influenced by Numerology, so it is taught that because there is a connection between the mathematical value of three times the name of God—YHVH—and that of the word "salt," we should dip our bread three times into salt when reciting a grace before meals.

It is also good to eat salt after a meal, because this protects against any harm. Eating bread and salt with your first meal upon moving into a new home will protect the house against evil spirits, and also represents the hope that food will never be lacking in the home. People also would keep some in their pocket to protect them against evil spirits.

Above: *Eating bread and salt with your first meal when moving into a new home protects against evil spirits, and also represents the hope of abundance.*

Below: *The letter Tzaddi stands for magnaminity.*

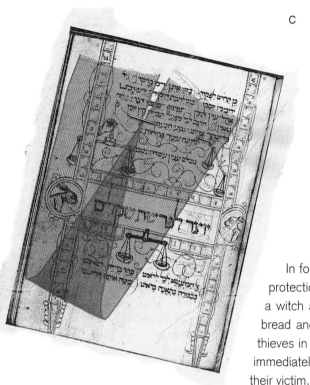

In folk superstition, salt and bread were often recommended as protection against witches, spirits, and magicians. It was said that if a witch attacked you but you forced her to give you some of her bread and salt, she would die. On the other hand, murderers and thieves in times gone by would eat a meal containing salt and bread immediately after a crime, in order to protect them from the spirit of their victim.

Salt is still considered to be extremely important in fighting evil today. Carrying around a pouch of salt will protect you against attacks from demons and the evil eye.

In order to spiritually cleanse your home or workplace, sprinkle salt water in the corners. For protection against bad vibes in the workplace, I always teach people to sprinkle salt across the entrance to their space. When buying crystals and gemstones, they should be first washed in sea salt to cleanse them of any bad vibes or memories that they may have picked up on their journey to you.

Above: *Wearing red ribbon is thought to protect life, as red represents blood, the lifeforce.*

WEARING RED RIBBON OR WOOL is probably one of the most ancient and well-known of Kabbalah traditions. Red is the color of blood, the physical lifeforce which flows through us. The wearing of red will protect us from all evil in either thought or actions.

Babies are thought to be particularly susceptible to the evil eye, and you should always pin a red ribbon to the diaper and sew some onto the baby's vest. My mother would be furious if ever she found any of my children without this attachment. She was born during the first quarter of the twentieth century, and many of her generation still wear their red ribbons attached to their underwear to protect them.

Today I teach many people who come to me for advice to wear either a red ribbon sewn onto their undergarments, or a piece of red wool tied around their wrists—the wool must be pure wool and not mixed with any synthetics. Quite an industry is growing up around this belief, and many people are making money by selling these articles as having been blessed at the Tombs of the Patriarchs or the Western Wall, and packaging them with a prayer. This is all very nice, but in fact it really does not matter where you get your wool or ribbon from, so long as it is red. It is, of course, always

pleasing to give the ribbon or wool as a gift with love and affection, because this will then help pass on your healing energies to the recipient.

Even more fascinating is the sudden appearance of many media personalities proudly displaying their red woolen bracelets for all to see. The important thing to remember is that it really does not matter where you wear the red amulet. My mother's and previous generations would always wear their red ribbon hidden, so that others did not know about it. My generation would also hide it, and many would laugh about "the old ways," and ignore their mother's and *bubba's* (grandmother's) advice. Now it is hip to be seen displaying this ancient form of protection as the new "in" thing!

Traditionally, many new mothers refuse to accept praises on behalf of an infant because they could come with a hidden jealous intent. They protect their child by placing the red ribbon on them, and also they will spit three times across the baby's head to push any evil intent back. These expressions come from a very ancient ritual that was passed down orally but today is mostly forgotten, which I print for the first time on page 69.

Above: *The letters Pei (top) and Ayin (below).*
Below: *Metal protects against evil spirits.*

Other Superstitions

ONE SUPERSTITION THAT is still popular today is that you should never sew, or have something sewn onto, a garment while you are wearing it. This is based on the old custom that the deceased are sewn into their burial shrouds, and you would not want demons to mistakenly think that you were dead. The only way around this is to chew on a piece of thread while someone is sewing something on to your garment, to show that you are very much alive.

Books should never be left open when you are finished with them, because an evil spirit can easily enter the written words and distort their meaning.

Metal has protective powers. Even today, people wear or carry safety pins to protect themselves.

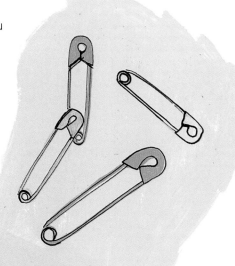

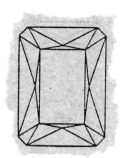

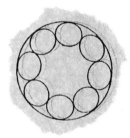

USING CRYSTALS AND GEMS

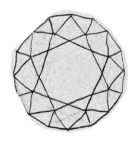

CRYSTALS AND GEMS have been used by nearly every civilization known to man for protection against demons, evil spirits, and the evil eye, and for healing since the beginning of our existence. Kabbalah is no different in encouraging their use, and they are spoken of many times in the Bible.

In Exodus 28:17–20, we read about the instructions directly from God of the layout of the twelve gemstones that are to be part of the vestments of the High Priest Aaron. They were to represent the twelve tribes of Israel and be engraved with their names. They are known as the *Urim* and *Thummim*. These crystals were used for psychic protection, enhancing the wisdom and healing powers of the High Priest, and in addition reputedly as a sacred means of divination.

There is a current revival in the knowledge of the power of crystals, and from what is understood, this breastplate must have been very powerful, due to the combination of the energies of the different crystals.

The following is a description of the gems in the order that they were laid out. To help you to understand the power of this garment, I have added a brief description of the attributed healing powers of each of the crystals.

Below: *The letter Samekh.*

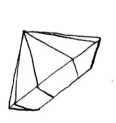

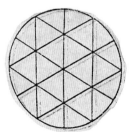

FIRST ROW

SARDIN Many presume that this is in fact *camelian*. Raises self-esteem and prevents self-destructive tendencies. Helps when making choices. Can help heal jealousy and envy, whether coming from within yourself, or from another person. Brings joy and energizes us to stimulate courage, self-confidence, ambition, assertiveness, and bringing ideas to fulfillment.

CHRYSOLITE The chrysolite known today is the olive-green silicate we call *peridot*. This crystal stimulates the mind, reduces stress, and accelerates personal growth.

GREEN FELDSPAR This was probably *amazonite*. Strengthens and balances the auric and mental bodies. Uplifting, helps you to feel good about yourself, and to let go of guilt and fear.

SECOND ROW

PURPLE GARNET A subtle guide to clarity and peace of mind. Guiding and centering. Brings focus and order, helps dissolve confusion.

LAPIS LAZULI An energizing, powerful amplifier of psychic abilities and communication with your higher self. Helps intellectual clarity, creativity, communication, and focus.

JADE Soothes, heals, and balances. Believed to promote a long and prosperous life. Encourages wisdom, clarity, and courage while balancing the emotions.

THIRD ROW

TURQUOISE Connects and vitalizes. Enhances love, communication, loyalty, and friendship. Encourages success and strength.

AGATE Balances, stabilizes, and protects. Brings a sense of courage and fortitude. Strengthens the mind and body. It is also believed to possess magical powers.

JASPER A very powerful all-around healer. Helps ground you physically and emotionally. Can assist and protect in dangerous situations. Helps one to remember and interpret dreams. This stone was used by Native American shamans for its protective and magical powers.

FOURTH ROW

TOPAZ Known as the stone of "true love and success in all aspirations." Promotes confidence in one's own abilities, creativity, and individuality. Replaces negativity with love and joyfulness.

CORNELIAN This is translated as meaning *onyx*, a powerful protector against negative energies, such as the evil eye. Helps banish grief, enhances self-control, guides one to wise decision-making, and helps attract happiness and prosperity.

GREEN JASPER A very powerful all-around healer. Conducive to spiritual awareness and insight. Also a strong protector against negative influences.

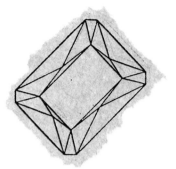

Other crystals used by Kabbalists for their powerful healing qualities include:

AMETHYST Stimulates intuition and psychic development by enhancing the development of tuning into our sixth sense, opening us up to God's energies. Relaxing, encourages tranquility, dissolves anxiety, helps insomnia, protects, purifies, and uplifts.

BERYL Opens one up to divine guidance and therefore to acts of purity and love.

CORAL Makes one spiritually aware by enhancing intuition, visualization, and imagination.

EMERALD Brings harmony and peace to one's life. Stimulates memory and intelligence. Opens one up to understanding the laws of creation and the cosmos.

QUARTZ The "all-singing, all-dancing" crystal. Amplifies, enhances, activates, and transmits energy. Enhances meditation and spiritual development. Disperses negative energy directed at us. A powerful all-around healer.

RUBY Brings spiritual wisdom, and helps one peacefully resolve conflicts and disputes. Protects against unhappiness, bad dreams, and lightning. Protects against all forms of psychic attack.

SAPPHIRE Opens the mind up to spirituality, intuition, and the beauty and wonder of the universe. Brings a radiant energy to our unconscious thoughts. Encourages our opening up to discourse with God.

THE KENANAH HORA

Below: *Meditating on the letter Nun strengthens faith.*

THIS IS THE MOST powerful counteractive measure that there is against the evil eye.

Although *kenanah hora* is Yiddish for "the evil eye," this ritual is in fact a very powerful form of healing of both the auric and physical bodies. The practice of this ritual was passed down through my father's family, with only one in each generation receiving the knowledge and being able to perform it.

As with all traditional Kabbalist practices, I was taught never to discuss this outside the immediate family. As a practicing healer, I have taught the method to a chosen few. Working with clairvoyants and healers, I have been

Above: *The Hebrew letters Tav (right) and Mem (left).*

told that this ritual is extremely ancient, probably pre-Egyptian in origin. Although it is very quick, it is also very powerful, and I always warn recipients that it can take twenty-four hours to work, and they must be prepared to go home and rest. The healing seems to take time to permeate slowly through the body, and the ritual also cleanses the aura. Traditionally, it will also send any evil intent back to where it has come from.

Although I use the words "lick" and "spit," the licks are in fact only light touches with the tongue (to draw any bad vibes into you), and the spits are the sound of spitting (to throw back out the vibes into the atmosphere) rather than big licks and spits.

- **Remove your shoes and feel the energies draw up through the earth.**
- **Stand opposite the receiver.**
- **Place your hands gently on the receiver's shoulders so that you can make contact.**
- **The receiver closes their eyes.**
- **Lick the left eye three times and spit three times in succession to the left of the head, aiming just past the ear.**
- **Repeat on the right eye and to the right side of the head.**
- **Lick the middle of the forehead—the area of the third eye—three times, and spit three times, aiming over the top of the head.**
- **Remove your hands from the recipient's shoulders. You may need to take a step back.**
- **Without touching the recipient, physically push away any bad vibes from the area at**
the side of the recipient's head three times. Be careful, because I have often found that people who are sensitive to healing can nearly topple over, even though you are not physically touching them.
- **Place your left hand on the left shoulder and the right hand on the right shoulder, and drag them quickly down to the end of the recipient's fingers and onward, pushing away any psychic debris that may remain. Repeat this three times.**
- **The ritual is now finished, and the recipient should be encouraged to sit for a few moments and then go home to rest. The immediate results of this technique can vary from a quick energy shock to the system to a sublime feeling of relaxation. Nearly always, fatigue overcomes the recipient within a short space of time.**

Above: *(Right to left) The Hebrew letters Kuf, Shin, and Resh.*

A QUICK NOTE ON THE REACTION to this ritual perhaps should be given as a warning. A couple of years after I was married, I asked my father to perform this ritual on my husband, Jeffrey, because I felt there were many bad vibes around him, too many things were going wrong. My husband had always laughed at my "gypsy" ways, as he called them.

After my father performed the ritual we went home, and Jeffrey felt very tired and went to bed. A few hours later my father phoned to ask how Jeffrey was, because he felt concerned, and warned me that because he had shifted a lot of bad energy, Jeffrey might be feeling quite ill, but not to worry—he would be all right in the morning. Sure enough, when I entered our bedroom Jeffrey was in bed, feeling very sorry for himself, with a raging temperature of 104 degrees. He admitted afterwards that although he had always laughed at my beliefs, he had lain in bed wondering what on earth had my father done to him. Needless to say, this experience completely changed his attitude!

THE SHEMA

HEAR O ISRAEL, THE LORD OUR GOD, THE LORD IS ONE

SHEMA YISRAEL, ADONAI ELOHEINU, ADONAI ECHAD

I WAS ALWAYS AWARE, even as a child, of the power of the prayer, the Shema. This prayer is the fundamental teaching of Judaism and therefore Kabbalah.

In the *Talmud* it is noted that the Shema has the unique power to protect against the forces of evil, and I was always instinctively aware that that the first line would protect me and give me a feeling of security, while at the same time bringing me closer to God. The full text of this prayer appears on page 107, but try to learn the first line by heart and repeat it silently as many times as you feel the need, especially when you want added protection.

יֹאמְרוּ הַגּוֹיִם אַיֵּה־נָא אֱלֹהֵיהֶם: וֵאלֹהֵינוּ בַשָּׁמָיִם כֹּל אֲשֶׁר־חָפֵץ
עָשָׂה: עֲצַבֵּיהֶם כֶּסֶף וְזָהָב מַעֲשֵׂה יְדֵי אָדָם: פֶּה־לָהֶם וְלֹא יְדַבֵּרוּ עֵינַיִם
לָהֶם וְלֹא יִרְאוּ: אָזְנַיִם לָהֶם וְלֹא יִשְׁמָעוּ אַף לָהֶם וְלֹא יְרִיחוּן: יְדֵיהֶם
וְלֹא יְמִישׁוּן רַגְלֵיהֶם וְלֹא יְהַלֵּכוּ לֹא־יֶהְגּוּ בִּגְרוֹנָם: כְּמוֹהֶם יִהְיוּ עֹשֵׂיהֶם
כֹּל אֲשֶׁר־בֹּטֵחַ בָּהֶם: יִשְׂרָאֵל בְּטַח בַּיי עֶזְרָם וּמָגִנָּם הוּא: בֵּית אַהֲרֹן
בִּטְחוּ בַיי עֶזְרָם וּמָגִנָּם הוּא: יִרְאֵי יי בִּטְחוּ בַיי עֶזְרָם וּמָגִנָּם הוּא:
יי זְכָרָנוּ יְבָרֵךְ יְבָרֵךְ אֶת־בֵּית יִשְׂרָאֵל יְבָרֵךְ אֶת־בֵּית אַהֲרֹן: יְבָרֵךְ
יִרְאֵי יי הַקְּטַנִּים עִם־הַגְּדֹלִים: יֹסֵף יי עֲלֵיכֶם עֲלֵיכֶם וְעַל־בְּנֵיכֶם:
בְּרוּכִים אַתֶּם לַיי עֹשֵׂה שָׁמַיִם וָאָרֶץ: הַשָּׁמַיִם שָׁמַיִם לַיי וְהָאָרֶץ נָתַן
נְבָרֵךְ

Kabbalah
for Healing

Kabbalah

FOR HEALING

HEALING AND THE TREE OF LIFE

HEALING IS A WORD that covers many different aspects within our own lives and within the world around us. Kabbalah teaches how to heal our physical bodies and our mental, emotional, and spiritual bodies as well. We are then taught to look beyond ourselves, and to heal on a planetary level.

THIS IS TRUE HEALING, as opposed to physical healing, which focuses on physical pain and illness. By focusing on our inner and spiritual levels of healing, we often find that our physical pain is helped enormously. This is often a way of treating the cause of the pain, as opposed to the symptom.

There are many ways of using Kabbalah for healing, and in the first part of this chapter we shall use the Tree of Life, which represents a map of our inner selves, including our emotions, personality, soul, and the reflection of ourselves that we show to the outside world.

In order to do this we must first understand the different energy levels of each of the Sephirot, and then how this energy can be harnessed to aid our development and healing process. This chapter will also explain how by using aids such as color, crystals, and the names of God, the energies of the Sephirot can be enhanced and amplified in order to aid personal and planetary healing.

The following is a chart of how the Sephirot relate to the whole person. This will make is easier for you to understand which particular Sephirah will help you with a particular problem.

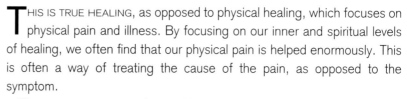

FROM THE COSMOS AND SEPHIROT TO MIND AND BODY

PERSON	COSMOS	SEPHIRAH	ASSOCIATION
SOUL	AIN SOF	KETER	SPIRITUALITY
SUBCONSCIOUS	ATZILUT	KETER	SPIRITUALITY
CONSCIOUS MIND	BERIYA	HOKHMAH	PURPOSE
		BINAH	AWARENESS
		DAAT	WISDOM
EMOTIONS	YETZIRA	HESSED	LOVE
		GEVURAH	WILL
		TIFERET	SELF
		NETZAH	FEELINGS
		HOD	THOUGHTS
		YESOD	SUBCONSCIOUS EMOTIONS
PHYSICAL BODY	ASSIYA	MALKHUT	PHYSICAL BODY AND SENSATIONS

KETER IS THE LINK between our subconscious mind, our soul, and our direct communication with the spiritual world. The main purpose of studying Kabbalah is to become an open channel with the spiritual realms and ultimately with God. By working with some of the meditations in this chapter you will find that your attitude and ability to tune into the spiritual realms will change, and eventually, with practice, you will find that you are able to work within the realms of Keter.

It is via the Sephirah Keter that spiritual healers are able to let through their spiritual guides.

Below: *The Hebrew letter Vav.*

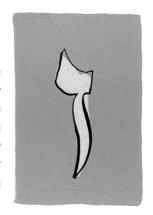

Changing How We Think and Feel

THIS SECTION EXPLAINS how the Sephirot can specifically help to formulate our emotional and mental states. This will guide you to understand how they can each help you to be aware of, and focus on any problems in these areas. At the same time they will help you to understand how and why you think the way you do, and make you very aware of your actions as seen by others. By concentrating and specifically working on certain aspects of your emotional and mental states, you will find that your whole outlook on life can change, and by this process how other people view you.

Above: *(Right to left) The letters Gimel, Daled, and Hei, which are numbered 3, 4, and 5 in the Hebrew alphabet.*

In order to change the ways in which we think and feel, we must learn to embrace and work with the Sephirotic "flows" through which we learn to connect with our inner selves, our soul, and thus onward with the cosmos.

Our emotions are the thoughts that we **feel**. They are often hard to describe in words, and we tend to use metaphors to convey them to others. We may tend to keep most of our thoughts to ourselves. We often expand on our thoughts in order to experience our lives and reality.

Our mentality is the way we **think**. It is the pathway through which our inner feelings and our soul express the thought processes through our brain to exit as words and actions.

The Sephirot of the Mind

THE FOLLOWING TWO Sephirot, Hokhmah and Binah, formulate our thought processes. With Daat, they are collectively known as the Seichel.

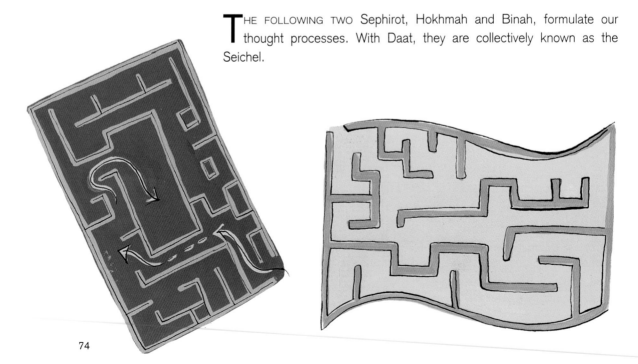

HOKHMAH – PURPOSE

THIS IS THE spiritual flow that is the source of our creativity, wisdom, and inspiration. It is through the channel of Hokhmah that our soul transforms the subconscious into conscious awareness.

By working on our Hokhmah flow, we can train ourselves to delve deeper into our subconscious levels in order to become more creative and questioning, and to see the world in a different way. By working with the Hokhmah flow, you can learn how to train yourself to reinterpret your own life and all that is around you. You can work on alleviating old fears and feelings of guilt, and progress onward to a life that is filled with joy, love, and happiness.

Above: *Hokhmah is concerned with understanding our spiritual source—going back to the seed of ourselves to transform awareness.*

A HOKHMAH EXERCISE

• Take a notepad and a pen or pencil and go to a quiet place where you will not be disturbed.

• Breathe easily and feel yourself relax.

• Think about something that comes into your mind—anything will do.

• Write that thought down as simply as possible.

• Think about the origin of that thought—where did it spring from?

• Now think about the contents of the thought—was it good, constructive, angry, or destructive?

• Relax and consciously decide to substitute that thought. Become aware of changing its construction. If it was an angry or destructive thought, take your time and work on it until you have managed to transform its negative aspects into positive ones.

THIS EXERCISE CAN be repeated as often as you wish. It demonstrates to you how you can control your thoughts and emotions by taking a moment to understand how your thoughts are formulated. It will also help you to understand how to train yourself to exercise a more balanced and logical aspect into your more angry thoughts.

Above: *Binah energy is the process of shaping the spiritual energy of Hokhmah (see p. 75).*

BINAH – AWARENESS

I T IS THROUGH THE FLOW of Binah that the creative current of Hokhmah takes on direction and becomes productive thought. Binah is the source that gives the thought process the guidance and direction to develop, analyze, and take shape.

In order to understand how the energy of Binah can be used, you must first become aware of how your thought process works. Take a moment and think about how you react to certain aspects of your life that are invariably repeated, such as having to speak regularly to someone who really grates on your nerves, or the stress of meeting monthly payments. These repetitive thoughts that give you feelings of trepidation and distress probably occur regularly both at home and at work—have you completed that particular report correctly, or have you reached your monthly targets?

These ways of thinking are the result of habits developed probably from early childhood. In order to use the flow of Binah correctly, we must first recognize these thinking habits, and then consciously decide to work on changing them. This process involves taking the flow of Hokhmah, which teaches us to understand how we can change our thought process, and redirecting it through our Binah flow of making us aware of *how* we are going to change the way we think.

Liken this process to buying a bag of potatoes. First you use your Hokhmah center to think about actually buying the potatoes, but it is your Binah flow that actually tells you how to cook them to make them edible.

By becoming aware of the workings of the Hokhmah thought process with the direction of Binah, you will be able to improve the way you feel about particular people or events, and ultimately change the way you think.

A BINAH EXERCISE

• Take yourself to a quiet place where you will not be disturbed. Sit comfortably and relax.

• Close your eyes and focus on your breathing until you feel truly relaxed.

• In your mind's eye slowly "see" your body and scan it slowly from your feet upwards.

• Become aware of your senses one by one—touch, smell, taste, seeing, and hearing.

• Rub your tongue over your teeth and the inside of your mouth, and taste them.

• Become aware of any smells around you.

• Let your fingertips touch each other—feel the sensation.

• Listen—what can you hear? The wind, the rain, the rustling of the trees, the traffic in the distance?

• Be aware of "seeing," even though your eyes are closed.

• Now relax further and let your thoughts freely flow in and out of your mind. Don't hold on to any thoughts, just let them flow and ebb, in and out of your mind.

• When you are ready, form the picture of a balloon in your mind.

• Now color it any color you like—this is your creation.

• Picture your weightless balloon floating through time and space to a wonderful place—this could be a beautiful, flower-filled garden with flowing waterfalls, or perhaps a meadow full of green, luscious grass intermingled with daisies and large yellow buttercups dancing in a gentle wind.

• Watch your balloon drifting through this landscape, being blown by a gentle breeze. This is your thought, and you can let it travel wherever you wish—you are in control of it.

• Journey with this thought balloon for as long as you like, and when you are finished let it gently come back down to earth.

• Repeat the exercise by forming another thought balloon in another color, and again control its journey through wherever you would like, just as with the first thought balloon.

• When you are ready, return to the first thought balloon, but this time become conscious of changing the surrounding landscape. Become aware of directing its journey exactly where you want it to travel along specific pathways and shortcuts. If there are certain aspects of the surrounding landscape that you are not comfortable with, change them to more pleasing features. This time you are more in control of your thought.

• When you want to finish this exercise, become aware of retracing your steps through your journey, perhaps using a different path or shortcut, and allow your thought balloon to close down by first losing its color and then watching it deflate and dissolve into nothingness.

• Become conscious of your breathing, and when you feel ready, open up your eyes.

• Repeat this exercise every day for a week, and you will find that you will become more aware of how your thoughts form, and how they can be controlled.

THE ULTIMATE AIM of this exercise is to teach you how you can change the direction of your thinking patterns and make them more adjustable and comforting. If, for example, you know that there are certain thoughts that make you uncomfortable or make you feel panicky, send them on their travels and find ways to control and redirect them.

DAAT – WISDOM

Above: *Daat represents our inside knowledge.*

THE MERGING ENERGIES of Hokhmah and Binah need the flow of Daat to develop the sequence that emerges as a "thought" in our mind. It is through Daat that we get that feeling of "knowing" that many call intuition.

The energy of Daat flows directly from Keter, the highest Sephirah and the one through which our soul energy is derived. This higher form of Daat is called *Da'at Elyon*, and allows us to tune into what many call our sixth sense. By combining the energy of the higher Daat with the energies of Hokhmah and Binah, our sixth sense allows us to have greater insight, more creativity, and understanding than those people who keep this energy closed down. It is only when we begin to rationalize these thoughts, or listen to others, that we begin to ignore them.

The lower form of Daat is known as *Da'at Tachton*, and it is through this that we combine the emotion of knowing something with our mind with the feeling and energy that flows from our heart. The powerful spiritual energy of Daat is an important contributory factor when learning to achieve greater spiritual knowledge, health, and wellbeing. It is through this energy that we can learn to change not only our own body chemistry, but also the way in which others perceive us. All the healing meditations in the next part of this chapter (see pages 79, 81, 82, 84, 85, 87) will link you with the spiritual and healing energy of Daat.

A DAAT EXERCISE

ONE OF THE THOUGHT processes which we encounter through Daat is that of inner peace, and the following is an easy exercise to tune into this state of mind.

• Take yourself to a quiet place. Sit comfortably so you can relax, and concentrate on your breathing.

• When you are ready, feel the divine, white, radiant light of Keter flow all over you from above your head, and then let it enter your body.

• Feel it bathe your body with its peaceful and caressing radiance as it gently dissolves all of your feelings of stress, anxiety, and tiredness.

• Feel it flow into every part of your being as it fills you with divine, spiritual peace.

• When you are ready, ask for any guidance or assistance that you may need in your life. Ask for the insight to make the right decisions to help you to become a wise and spiritually advanced person in this lifetime.

• When you feel ready, consciously let the divine energy drain from your body and the space around you. Sit quietly for a few moments, reliving the peace that surrounded you, before slowly standing up and getting on with your life.

The Sephirot of Emotion

IT IS THROUGH the seven following Sephirot, the Middot, that our inner feelings develop and are controlled and guided.

HESSED – MERCY

HESSED IS THE FLOW that lets us experience feelings and free will, but we should always be aware that feelings and free will without a sense of direction can become emotionally draining. For this reason Hessed must be guided by the mind flow of Daat.

It is through Hessed that we experience the emotion of giving and sharing. It stops us from being self-centered, and teaches us to care and think about others. This in turn helps us to communicate with those around us, leading us to friendship and personal fulfillment.

Above: *Hessed is the energy of compassion.*

A HESSED EXERCISE

THIS EXERCISE IS ABOUT giving out a little of your love and compassion to those around you.

• Go to a quiet place, sit in a comfortable chair, remove your shoes, relax, and close your eyes.
• Feel the soles of your feet making contact with the floor.
• Concentrate on your breathing until you feel totally relaxed.
• Feel yourself open up to the love and healing powers of the universe, and starting with your feet, feel the energy flow up your body, eventually filling every part of your being.
• When you are ready, think of all your loved ones, friends, and acquaintances. Send out your love and healing energy to them.
• Try to picture them receiving this energy.
• Feel them bathe in this spiritual healing energy, which is filled with your love.
• Now—and this is the hard part—if there is someone whom you dislike or have had a disagreement with, send them out healing and loving thoughts.
• Now send out your love to the whole planet and visualize all the damage we are doing to it being gently healed.
• When you are ready, concentrate on your breathing again, and move ever onward.

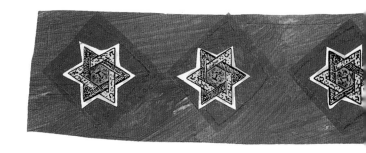

GEVURAH – JUDGMENT

Above: *Gevurah is about focusing our minds to achieve goals and communicate decisions.*

THE HESSED FLOW of our feelings is balanced and guided by the opposite position of Gevurah. This emotion helps control and restrict our choices by helping us focus on what is best for us.

The energy of the Sephirah of Gevurah is the flow that controls our inner, and often our outer strength. It is upon Gevurah that we should meditate when we wish to enhance our use of willpower and conviction. Gevurah directs our mental energies into being able to concentrate and focus on problems and goals, and gives our spiritual energy a defined shape. By this I mean that the next time you lift your groceries out of your car and you become aware of your muscles tightening, you are using the energy of Gevurah.

Gevurah is also the root of discipline for both our mind and our physical body. It is through Gevurah that we achieve self-control and self-mastery, and it is therefore through Gevurah that we learn to discipline ourselves to learn, study, and master whatever we strive to.

Although in some ways we must be self-centered when seeking to achieve mastery over whatever we seek, such as academic honors, or pure self-discipline in a work-related environment, we must also look to the Sephirah of Gevurah to enable us to become other-centered when setting out to achieve our goals.

As mentioned in the previous chapter, all the Sephirot must be balanced by their opposite Sephirot on the Tree of Life. On the opposite side to Gevurah is the balance of Hessed, and this is very important, because without this balance Gevurah can be hurtful and, in some cases, destructive. It is through Gevurah that anger manifests itself, sometimes exploding into violence. This can be expressed by some of the following examples:

- Exploding with violent words or actions.
- Building up inner resentment about a situation, leading to thoughts of revenge.
- Road rage.

- Anger at people who put pressure on you at work—perhaps by insisting on almost impossible deadlines.
- Threats to your self-esteem by feeling humiliated by words or actions of others.

IN ADDITION, by tuning into Gevurah without the counterbalance of Hessed one can become manipulative and egotistic, becoming determined to get one's own way, no matter who gets hurt in the progress. We must therefore contemplate on Gevurah as the source of self-discipline and self-control, at the same time being aware of the feelings of the people around us, and ultimately with the goal of achieving a spiritual unity with God.

Right: *The Hebrew letters
Aleph (far right) and
Beit (right).*

A GEVURAH EXERCISE

• Take yourself to a quiet place, close your eyes, relax, and either sit comfortably or lie down.

• Concentrate on your breathing.

• When you are ready, imagine a shaft of white, brilliant light flowing into the top of your head through your crown.

• As it passes through your head, let the color now change to red, and let it fill the whole of your body.

• Intone to yourself the divine name ELOHIM GIBOR a number of times.

• Ask for the help and guidance that you require, or just to become a part of the global spiritual enlightenment that is happening all around us on a planetary level.

• Feel the divine guidance pour through you, and feel at peace with yourself.

• When you are ready, let the red light flow back up to your head.

• Let the white shaft return from whence it came.

ELOHIM GIBOR

Above: *Tiferet is concerned with accepting difference and seeing the best in people.*

TIFERET—BEAUTY AND COMPASSION

THE CENTRAL POSITION of Tiferet helps to balance the opposite emotions of Hessed—giving in to our feelings—and Gevurah—controlling our feelings. For this important reason it is through Tiferet that we seek to achieve inner balance.

Our individual gifts are often out of balance, and we therefore need to concentrate on the Sephirah of Tiferet to balance them. For example, someone may be extremely practical, but may be uncaring and scathing about other people's opinions and needs.

Our inner Sephirah of Tiferet may need rebalancing, in order to allow us to understand and allow for other people's weaknesses. We need the balance of the emotions of caring and compassion within our lives. If we do not achieve balance between our giving and taking emotions, we could find ourselves with feelings of emotional chaos.

We must learn to feel compassion for others by making a point of trying to understand how others come to their opinions, or act the way that they do. Without compassion in our lives, we would all become bitter and disillusioned.

A TIFERET EXERCISE

• Take yourself to a quiet place, sit comfortably, close your eyes, and relax.

• Imagine that you are walking up four stairs and reaching an open doorway.

• Go through the doorway into a beautiful garden full of flowers, or perhaps into an open pasture full of young lambs dancing in the warm sunlight.

• Feel the sunlight gently warming you as you walk along.

• Now see some of your friends and acquaintances walking towards you.

• Greet them and feel their friendship and warmth reaching out to you.

• Now return this friendship by reaching out with your own feelings of love, joy, and appreciation of their companionship.

• Feel this open, two-way communication as the energy of true friendship passes between you.

• Be aware that everyone thinks and acts differently, and that is what makes us all so special.

• Be aware that you can learn much from the experiences of others, and that you must also sometimes make allowances for their faults—no one is perfect.

• Be aware that in order to fulfill our place on this planet we must live with many different people around us, and each one is special and unique. Most importantly, each one has been created by God.

• Enjoy these feelings, and when you are ready, return through the doorway, back down the four stairs, and move onward with your life.

EXTERNAL EMOTIONS

IN ORDER TO externalize the previous emotions, we need the influence of the following three Sephirot, which help present our "personality" to the world around us.

NETZAH—ETERNITY

ONCE OUR INTERNAL emotions are sorted out, we need the flow of Netzah to enable them to be communicated to the outside world, either by relationships or conversation. The "victory" of Netzah is actually the accomplishment of being able to let our emotions reach out from within ourselves to the boundaries beyond, to be able to form and hold on to meaningful relationships.

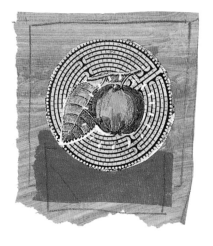

It is through the flow of Netzah that we go beyond the "me" mentality and reach out to others. From a young age we are very aware of being locked within our own inner world, and yearn to investigate and form friendships and relationships in the world around us. It is the flow of Netzah that encourages us to take that step into the world outside ourselves.

Most of us have found that it is not easy to take this step, and often our overtures of friendship are rebutted, sometimes in a cruel way, but we all keep on exploring and pushing ourselves, and eventually most of us find that, perhaps with a little work, we begin to find the companionship we require. We must be careful, however, that—perhaps due to disappointment or discomfort when we take our early tentative steps to reaching out to others—we find that our Netzah flow has become stunted.

Above: *Netzah focuses on taking the risk of expressing love to others and acting from the heart.*

By utilizing the experience of our feelings—Hessed together with the balance of Tiferet—it is through the Sephirah of Netzah that we can extend our egotistic confines to sending out feelings and love to other people. In other words, you learn to feel for others what you would that they would feel for you. This is where the emotion of love springs from.

As with other Sephirotic flows, Netzah must be carefully balanced so that it causes no harm. Bossiness, aggressiveness, and domination are just some of the negative aspects that spring to mind, which can be due to the Netzah flow being too powerful and strong. In other words, one may not just be extending one's ego boundaries outward, but may be actively trying to control others in their environment.

Below: *The letter Lamed.*

By working through the healing exercises in this book, you will become aware of how you can tone down the negative aspects of Netzah within your own personality. Even more important are the following ways in which you can protect yourself from those around you who are pushing their negative Netzah energies too close to your personal boundaries than is comfortable.

Above: *The letter Kaph.*
Left: *The Netzah exercise uses a mirror to deflect negative energies.*

NETZAH EXERCISES TO PROTECT YOU FROM THE NEGATIVE NETZAH FLOW OF OTHERS

• When you are either going to see or speak to the person who you feel tries to dominate you, imagine that you are enclosed within a bubble of color—any color you wish, but gold and silver are probably best. Now, when you see or speak to them, imagine that they cannot penetrate this protective bubble, and therefore cannot affect you.

• Imagine a mirror between yourself and that person so that you deflect their negative aspects back to them and away from you.

• When speaking to them, cover the area of your solar plexus with your hand to protect you from their negative influences, and to put you in charge of the situation.

• Wear either red ribbon or wool attached to one of your undergarments, or a bracelet of red wool on your wrist to protect you against negativity and bad vibes.

• Sprinkle some salt across the threshold of your workspace to prevent any negativity from entering your environment.

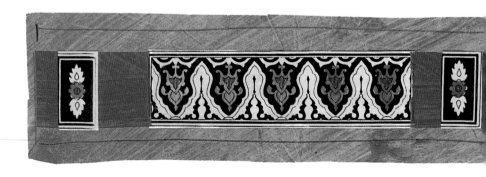

HOD—REVERBERATION

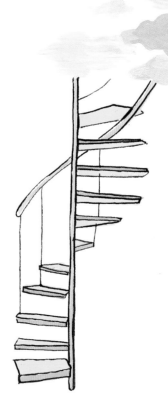

A S WE HAVE BEEN able to reach out to others by using the flow of Netzah, now, through the flow of Hod, we learn to understand and accommodate the feelings and emotions of others. This is the Sephirah that focuses on human relationships. If we find that we give our Netzah flow to someone but receive very little or nothing in return, then they are not allowing their outgoing energy of Hod to flow back to us. Many of us easily become aware of this feeling of being unable to communicate with someone, or a feeling that they are on a different wavelength. We should then be aware that we have no basis for an emotional relationship.

It is through Hod that we build up the feelings of trust and confidence within others toward ourselves. It is the balancing Sephirah to Netzah and can therefore control its negative aspects. It can also teach us the skill of holding a two-way dialogue. Through Hod we learn to listen to what others want from us on all levels, whether in our personal or our working lives.

Hod also teaches us about accepting both our own personal worth and that of others. We learn that instead of wallowing in disappointment and self-pity, we should take a step back and turn any painful experience into something positive that we can learn from. Through Hod we begin to understand that there is a reason for everything, and in common with many spiritual philosophies, we should see what we can learn from any setback as we climb the stairway of life.

A HOD EXERCISE

• Take a moment in a quiet place, and sit comfortably.

• Concentrate on your breathing until you feel relaxed.

• Think back to the last time that you felt truly happy.

• Bathe in the feelings of how good you felt, and bathe in the feeling of pleasure.

• Now take a moment and feel really good about yourself.

• Free yourself from any guilt or negative thoughts—what is past is past and cannot be undone, just be willing to learn from any past mistakes.

• You are one of God's magnificent creations, and you have the power within you to transcend any negativity that is thrown in your pathway. You are great, you are unique, and you are loved.

Above: *The letters Yod (top) and Tet (bottom). Together, they represent positive change.*

YESOD—FOUNDATION

Y ESOD IS THE CHANNEL through which all of the Sephirot of the mind and emotions flow when we are communicating with the outside world. It controls the nature and strength of all communication, especially between people. When we feel a close bond—a full sense of communication—with another person, it is because we have formed a Yesod bond with that person. Through Yesod flows the energies of Netzah, which progresses us from loneliness to relationships, and is balanced by the restraint of Hod.

It is through Yesod that we develop the qualities of intent—*kavannah*. We develop the way that we want to focus our minds with attributes of finding our true purpose in life and going full speed ahead and achieving this. The energy of this Sephirah also encompasses our capacity to give and take in relationships, and also to extend the depths of feelings and compassion that we extend to those beyond ourselves.

A YESOD EXERCISE

AN IMPORTANT ASPECT of Yesod is to strengthen our own feelings of adequacy and wholeness. The continuous realization of the divine presence is the key element in experiencing the kind of life that we desire. When you consistently surround yourself with a spiritual atmosphere, you align your inner being with clarity, balance, and understanding.

Fulfillment, peace, joy, and abundance are all available to you when you consciously embrace these ideas, constructively directing your thoughts through affirmations. Find one that speaks to you at that moment, and finally close your eyes, meditate deeply upon its meaning, and let it become a part of you.

• I close my eyes and open my heart up to the experience of my inner strength. I have the power to meet all that life throws at me.

• I close my eyes and open up to the healing energy of the universe. I feel its love and compassion as it fills me with its divine strength and light.

• I give thanks to God, who created me for my ability to create the life I deserve through my unique ability to think, love, and just be.

• I am where I am meant to be at this moment in my life. I have learned many lessons from my past experiences. I see all around me the glories of God's creation, and celebrate my connection to all life, and feel at peace and in harmony with being a part of this world

• I close my eyes and gently relax. I become aware of the essence of my soul within my physical body. I feel its light and energy, and know that I am filled with wisdom and God's love. I am truly a testimony to the miracle of creation, and know that I am truly loved.

• Every day I learn something new. I am full of positivity and well-being. Every day I am eager to seek out new experiences. All is well in my world, as from these experiences I will develop and grow.

• I approve of myself as my life ebbs and flows with change. I am in full control of my destiny, and choose to make every day wonderful.

• I close my eyes and take a moment to reflect on the success of the many events and projects in my life. I am always aware of the divine energy reflected in my soul and know that my life is a book already written, and I am forever learning lessons that are preordained.

• My life is abundant with the gifts from God. I am blessed with confidence, health, love, creativity, and am special and unique. I am a beautiful package that has been specially created by God. I thank God for my life, and will meet every problem which may be thrown at me with the knowledge that this is part of the learning curve of life, and I will overcome any obstacle put in my pathway.

• My life is whole and complete, and I love myself and am filled with harmony and balance. The more love and compassion that I give out to others, the more I shall receive in return. My inner capacity for this is endless, and others feel this when I greet them. I feel nourished when they return these feelings of love and compassion, and bathe in their energy and joy.

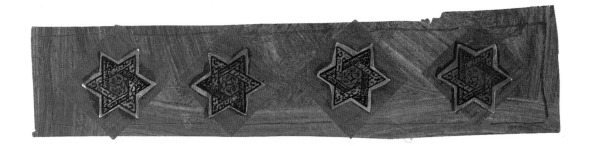

THE SEPHIROT OF RELATIONSHIPS

HOKHMAH is the source of our thoughts, creativity, and inspiration.

BINAH transforms them into coherent thought patterns, making us aware of how we feel and think.

DAAT combines the two with wisdom, giving birth to emotions.

HESSED teaches us how to experience our feelings, and promotes giving and sharing.

GEVURAH helps us to control this flow so that we know what is best for us.

TIFERET blends and balances our feelings so that we can understand the needs of others.

NETZAH helps us reach out to form meaningful relationships, love, and passion.

HOD enables us to have empathy with others. It is the key to communication.

HEALING THE PHYSICAL BODY

MALKHUT—KINGDOM

THIS IS THE FOCUS POINT of all Sephirot flows as they reach their final destination—man. All the emotions and thoughts that have flowed through from the Creator through our unconscious and conscious states are now firmly rooted in our physical make-up. This is how we see and think about everything and everybody, and how we in turn are perceived.

In the traditional literature of Kabbalah, great importance is placed upon the interaction between the supernal Sephirot and the physical attributes of the human body flowing directly from God through to the physical planes.

KETER manifests itself as the skull, which suggests that this is from where our conscious experiences emanate. It is through the physical attributes of Keter that our mental abilities expand and inflate.

HOKHMAH is deemed to be the seat of our mental prowess, or "the mind within the mind." **BINAH** is relative to Hokhmah in that it not only is attributed

to the physical heart, but also to the emotive one—the center of emotive experience emanating from the understanding of the mind. This is also further illustrated in the body, where Hokhmah is centered in the left lobe of the brain and Binah in the right lobe. The rear lobe of the brain is the center of **DAAT**, and it is at this point that the brain meets the spine.

HESSED embodies the left arm, and **GEVURAH** the right. This alludes to the Kabbalist saying, "Let the left arm push away and the right arm draw near." In this context, "push away" means to extricate, allowing the other party a feeling of independence, while "drawing near" illustrates the consciousness of interdependency. The balancing position of **TIFERET** manifests itself in the whole of the outer body and is centered between the arms in the torso.

NETZAH and **HOD** correspond to the legs, which represent the premier and most continual contact with the outer reality. They control the movement of the body as a whole, taking a person to where they wish to go. Hod is the energy that allows us to put one's best foot forward in a decisive manner. Netzah, centered in the left leg, helps control our movements by monitoring our decisive thrust.

YESOD is referred to as the "sign of the Holy Covenant" that corresponds to the male and female reproductive organs. Yesod is the body's physical manifestation of its own ability to authenticate and fulfill itself, as well as to communicate with others.

MALKHUT is where the power of the soul manifests itself in the mouth, which is the center of a person's power of influence. It is written "the word of the king's rules," meaning that the scope of the king's rule is marked by the extent of how far his word travels. It is the ability of the mouth to speak, to invoke one's powers of self-expression and thought, that in turn can affect one's world

Through the kingdom of Malkhut we are able to heal our physical body. When using the energy of this Sephirah by incorporating the additional energies of working with color and vibration, we can greatly enhance our healing abilities.

Above left: *The letter Chet represents guidance.*

Below: *The letter Zayin represents unity and soulfulness.*

Above: *(Right to left) The letters Ayin, Pei, and Tzaddi.*

Working With Color

WHEN YOU WORK on the Tree of Life, by adding the use of color you are in fact adding a potent energy force. By visualizing the color associated with each Sephirah, you are fine-tuning the energy of the Sephirot for use in a more precise manner.

When using color, it is a good idea to perhaps surround yourself with objects of the chosen color. This could include holding crystals, placing the correct color flowers near you, or wearing something in the correct color on the part of the body you wish to work on.

There are various color scales associated with The Tree of Life. Some use the colors attributed to the Sephirot, which change as they flow through the Four Worlds, and are illustrated in the chart opposite. The most regularly used colors are the King Scale and the Queen Scale. Through these scales we find, via the symbolism of color, the masculine and feminine aspects that co-exist within each Sephirah at all times.

The King Scale is deemed masculine and therefore has particular male attributes, making it stimulating, active, and outgoing. The Queen Scale is often thought of as feminine—receptive, open, and passive.

Most color diagrams of the Tree of Life show the Sephirot illustrated with their Queen Scale colors, because in general the Sephirot are seen as having more feminine characteristics, although they are open channels to the energies that flow through them directly from God, Who contains both feminine and masculine attributes.

THE COLOR SCALES

SEPHIRAH	KING SCALE	QUEEN SCALE
KETER	BRILLIANT WHITE	BRILLIANT WHITE
HOKHMAH	SOFT BLUE	GRAY
BINAH	CRIMSON	BLACK
DAAT	LAVENDER	GRAY-WHITE
HESSED	DEEP VIOLET	BLUE
GEVURAH	ORANGE	RED
TIFERET	ROSE PINK	YELLOW
NETZAH	AMBER	GREEN
HOD	VIOLET	ORANGE
YESOD	INDIGO	VIOLET
MALKHUT	YELLOW	CITRINE, RUSSET, OLIVE, BLACK

Vibrational Levels

CERTAIN NAMES OF GOD are associated with the various energies of each Sephirah when they are properly intoned and therefore vibrated. These names have never changed since they were used by the first Kabbalists, and the energies contained therein are our connection with the divine, both within our own psyche and in our place in the universe.

It is only now that people are becoming aware of the power of vibrational energy, which is often called *harmonic resonance*. This can be explained that if one object vibrates strongly it can influence another object nearby, which may share the same vibratory levels to also vibrate or resonate.

In order to intone correctly the names of God, you must first concentrate on the name, and then practice intoning it in such a way that you feel it resonate throughout your chest cavity and, with practice, throughout your whole body.

Left: *The letter Samekh.*

HEALING MEDITATIONS WITH SPECIFIC SEPHIRAH

THE FOLLOWING ARE some of the attributes of the individual Sephirah that you may wish to concentrate on when meditating:

KETER Spirituality, peace, relaxation, tranquility, illumination.

HOKHMAH Intuition, energy, vitality, creativity, wisdom, inspiration.

BINAH Strength and understanding of sorrow, faith, understanding, awareness, productive thought.

DAAT Wisdom in all matters, intuition, spiritual development, wellbeing.

HESSED Abundance, prosperity, generosity, fairness, sharing, inner feelings, communication, personal fulfillment.

GEVURAH Courage, fortitude, strength, change, energy, judgment, self-control, moving on, cleansing.

TIFERET Illumination, harmony, healing, success, compassion, fulfillment, inner balance, compassion, healing.

NETZAH Love and passion, meaningful relationships, creativity, idealism, social consciousness.

HOD Communication, learning, intuition, positivity, commerce.

YESOD Self-worth, positivity, confidence, focus, independence, psychic abilities.

MALKHUT Physical health, environment, self-discovery, environment.

YOU MAY WISH to concentrate on only one or two of the Sephirotic flows when you meditate, and this is entirely possible.

Left: *The letters Mem (left) and Nun (far left).*

GENERAL INSTRUCTIONS FOR INDIVIDUAL MEDITATIONS

• Take yourself to a quiet place where you will not be disturbed, and either sit comfortably or lie down. Close your eyes.

• Concentrate on your breathing.

• Imagine a shaft of pure, brilliant white light enter your realm of Keter, at the crown of your head. Intone to yourself the sacred name EHEYEH (Eh-hey-yah).

• Direct the shaft of light to the Sephirah you wish to concentrate on.

• Open up your individual Sephirah by using the colors and divine names below.

• Concentrate on how you want to open and use the flows of each of the Sephirot you are working on:

KETER	CROWN	BRILLIANT WHITE LIGHT	EHEYEH
HOKHMAH	LEFT TEMPLE	GRAY LIGHT	YAH
BINAH	RIGHT TEMPLE	BLACK LIGHT	YHVH ELOHIM
DAAT	BACK OF HEAD	GRAY-WHITE LIGHT	YHVH ELOHIM
HESSED	LEFT SHOULDER	BLUE LIGHT	EL
GEVURAH	RIGHT SHOULDER	RED LIGHT	ELOHIM GIBOR
TIFERET	HEART	YELLOW LIGHT	YHVH ELOAH VE DA'AT
NETZAH	LEFT HIP	GREEN LIGHT	YHVH TZABA'OT
HOD	RIGHT HIP	ORANGE LIGHT	ELOHIM TZABA'OT
YESOD	GENITAL REGION	VIOLET LIGHT	SHADDAI EL CHAI
MALKHUT	FEET AND ANKLES	CITRINE, RUSSET BROWN, BLACK, OLIVE-GREEN LIGHTS	ADONAI HA'ARETZ

• When you are finished, redirect the shaft of white light back through your body and up through Keter.

• Become aware of your breathing, and when you are ready, get up and get on with your life.

MEDITATION AND KABBALAH

MEDITATION IS THE DISCIPLINE by which we control the mind to think in a controlled manner for a period of time. It sounds a lot easier than it is, because when we begin to learn to meditate, the more we try to control our thoughts, the more they seem to be out of control. Try the exercise below as a first one:

HEALING ENERGIES

THIS CHART SHOWS THE HEALING ENERGIES OF THE TWENTY-TWO PATHWAYS WHICH CONNECT THE SEPHIROT INCLUDING THE CORRESPONDING COLOR AND SUGGESTED CRYSTALS WHICH SHOULD BE PART OF THE MEDITATION ON THIS PATHWAY

PATHWAY NUMBER	NO LINKING	LINKING	ASSOCIATED COLOR
11	KETER AND HOKHMAH	1 AND 2	EMERALD
12	KETER AND BINAH	1 AND 3	PURPLE
13	KETER AND TIFERET	1 AND 6	SILVER
14	HOKHMAH AND BINAH	2 AND 3	PINK
15	HOKHMAH AND TIFERET	2 AND 6	RED
16	HOKHMAH AND HESSED	2 AND 4	BROWN
17	BINAH AND TIFERET	3 AND 6	MAUVE
18	BINAH AND GEVURAH	3 AND 5	MAROON
19	HESSED AND GEVURAH	4 AND 5	DEEP PURPLE
20	HESSED AND TIFERET	4 AND 6	PLUM
21	HESSED AND NETZAH	4 AND 7	DARK BLUE
22	GEVURAH AND TIFERET	5 AND 6	PALE GREEN
23	GEVURAH AND HOD	5 AND 8	PALE PURPLE
24	TIFERET AND NETZAH	6 AND 7	INDIGO
25	TIFERET AND YESOD	6 AND 9	DARK BLUE
26	TIFERET AND HOD	6 AND 8	BLACK
27	NETZAH AND HOD	7 AND 8	BRIGHT RED
28	NETZAH AND YESOD	7 AND 9	MAUVE
29	NETZAH AND MALKHUT	7 AND 10	STONE
30	HOD AND YESOD	8 AND 9	GOLDEN YELLOW
31	HOD AND MALKHUT	8 AND 10	VERMILLION
32	YESOD AND MALKHUT	9 AND 10	WHITE, RED, YELLOW, BLUE

STOP THINKING

TRYING TO BLANK OUT your mind for a few moments and not think of anything else is not that easy—how long did it last? Unless you are experienced at meditation, you probably could not keep your mind empty of thoughts for more than a few seconds. Thoughts such as "I'm trying not to think" probably jumped into your mind. This is an example of how difficult it actually is to turn off your thoughts and to control your mind.

Another simple exercise is to relax and close your eyes. You may at first see flashes of light or images, but as these subside other images will take their place, which will change with no conscious help from you.

HUMAN BODY PARTS	SUGGESTED CRYSTALS
LEFT EYE, PITUITARY GLANDS	TOPAZ, CHALCEDONY JADE
RIGHT EYE, EAR, PINEAL	AGATE, OPAL, JADE
SPINAL CORD	MOONSTONE, QUARTZ, PEARL
MOUTH, NOSE	EMERALD, TURQUOISE
BLOOD IN ARTERIES	TOPAZ, CARNELIAN
PITUITARY SYSTEM	TOURMALINE, ALEXANDRITE
BLOOD IN VEINS	AMETHYST
PITUITARY SYSTEM	AMBER, CAT'S EYE
SPLEEN, LYMPHATIC SYSTEM	ROSE QUARTZ, AGATE, CALCITE, HEMATITE, AMBER, CAT'S EYE
LEFT LUNG	PERIDOT, CHRYSOCOLLA
RECTUM, LARGE INTESTINE	AMETHYST, LAPIS LAZULI, TIGER EYE
RIGHT LUNG	EMERALD, CHRYSOCOLLA
LARGE INTESTINE	AQUAMARINE, TIGER EYE
STOMACH	AGATE, DIOPTASE, PYRITE
SPINAL CORD AND SOLAR PLEXUS	SODALITE, CALCITE, CITRINE
PANCREAS, GALL BLADDER, LIVER	AGATE, BLACK ONYX, MALACHITE, JASPER, CITRINE
SMALL INTESTINES	RUBY, GARNET, CITRINE
MALE—LEFT TESTICLE, FEMALE—LEFT UTERINE TUBE AND OVARIES	QUARTZ, BLOODSTONE, ROSE QUARTZ, JADE, MOONSTONE
LEFT PART OF SKELETAL BONE STRUCTURE AND MUSCLES	BLOODSTONE, LAPIS LAZULI, PEARL, AVENTURINE
MALE—RIGHT TESTICLE, FEMALE—RIGHT UTERINE TUBE AND OVARIES	CHRYSOLITE, GOLD, BLOODSTONE, ROSE QUARTZ, JADE, MOONSTONE
RIGHT PART OF SKELETAL BONE STRUCTURE AND MUSCLES	BLOODSTONE, LAPIS LAZULI, FIRE OPAL, AVENTURINE
SKIN, BLADDER	ONYX, GYPSUM, JASPER

Now, still with your eyes closed, try to control these images. Try to see a round ball in your mind's eye, and try to control it bouncing up and down. You will find that unless you are experienced with this technique, it is impossible to control this image for any length of time. In Kabbalistic meditation this technique of controlling an image in the mind's eye is called "engraving," and can be achieved with practice and patience.

What these exercises demonstrate are that there are two parts of the mind—the conscious and the subconscious. The conscious part of the mind is controlled by your will, while the subconscious is not. One of the primary goals of meditation is to learn to control your subconscious mind, and in order to do this you must first control your conscious mind.

Most forms of meditation begin with the discipline of breathing control through exercises. This is because breathing is usually an automatic function that is controlled by your unconscious mind. Therefore, by controlling your breathing as you enter a meditative state, you are learning how to control the crossover situation from your conscious to your unconscious mind.

For most people who wish to participate in meditation, their aim is to reach "higher states of consciousness." This is a difficult state to define and describe. Put simply, we are aiming to enter into a state where we use parts of the mind to which we have no conscious access.

Below: *The letter Tav.*

References to meditation are to be found in major Kabbalist texts, from biblical times to the present day. Up to the Middle Ages, copious amounts of Kabbalist literature were written referring to meditation and meditative experiences, but the techniques used, although alluded to, were never actually described, leading one to the conclusion that this subject matter was the focus of an oral tradition of teaching Kabbalah. It was not until Abraham Abulafia (1240–96) wrote about the methods used in Kabbalistic meditation that anything appeared in writing.

The reason why this is one of the least-known aspects of Kabbalah is because although until the mid-nineteenth century meditation and mysticism were an important part of Judaism and therefore Kabbalah,

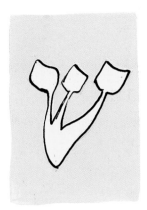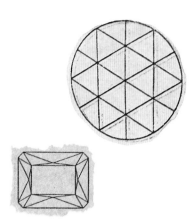

Above: *(Right to left) The letters Kuf, Resh, and Shin.*

during the last century and a half or so, much has been done to raise the intellectual level of knowledge, and therefore anything touching upon the mystical or magical, such as meditation, was pushed aside and ignored. The last couple of hundred years or so was also the time of great change in the study of Kabbalah. On the one hand you had the emigrants to the USA and parts of Europe, actively trying to assimilate into their new homelands, while on the other hand those Jews left in Russia and Poland had to deal with oppression, pogroms, and wars, including the tragedy of the Holocaust.

Therefore, due to a myriad of reasons, all references to meditation seem to have disappeared from mainstream Jewish literature and teachings about a hundred and fifty years ago.

In Kabbalah one's normal way of producing thoughts is referred to as *mochin de-katnuth*—the "mentality of childhood." It is only through meditation that we can progress beyond the way of thinking as a child into "adult thought."

KAVANNAH is the most common word used in Kabbalah to describe a form of meditation. This Hebrew word means meditation with "directed consciousness" or focus—in other words, when you meditate you should do so with a particular reason or goal in mind.

HITBONENUTH is another Hebrew term associated with Kabbalah and meditation. Literally translated, this means "self-understanding," and different results are achieved than those meditations based on Kavannah. By using the method of Hitbonenuth, you can focus on either an object or a thought and let this occupy your whole mind, allowing it to become the means to understanding yourself.

EXTERNALLY DIRECTED MEDITATION is a method that uses an external object to focus the mind in order to reach the higher states of consciousness. The object, which can be the focus of this type of meditation, could be anything, but is often a crystal, flower, picture, or lit candle. This type of meditation can be structured or unstructured—the choice is yours. If you decide on unstructured, allow yourself to focus on an object and let your

Above: *(Right to left) The letters Hei and Zayzin.*

thoughts flow freely through your mind. If you wish to structure this type of meditation, try to clear your mind completely and control your thoughts.

Whichever way you wish to structure this type of meditation, as you look deeper and deeper into the object of your focus, you will eventually begin to see its inner essence, and this will help banish all other thoughts from your mind. As you concentrate, you will eventually be able to see the divine in the object, and by focusing on this you will be able to open up completely to communicate with spiritual realms.

Below: *During the spiritual healing meditation, you allow yourself to become a vessel through which healing energies flow.*

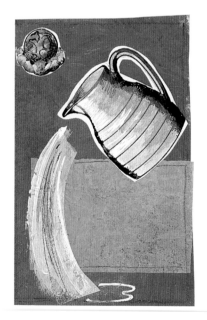

REMEMBER TO TAKE your time to close down after any type of meditation, or you could find yourself open to all sorts of outside influences, such as the feelings of people around you. Also, if you have lit a candle, remember to never leave it unattended.

Meditation for Spiritual Healing

THIS MEDITATION WILL allow you to become a vessel through which spiritual energies can flow and allow you to use their healing capabilities. With time and practice, this powerful meditation will allow you to become an open channel through which the healing spiritual energies of the cosmos will connect with your soul (*neshamah*) through the realm of Atzilut.

This can be used as a personal or a group meditation. You may wish to pre-record the steps. If you are using this for a group meditation, again this could be pre-recorded, or one member of the group could lead the other members through the different stages. When used for a group meditation, the sound of the group breathing in unison will help connect and focus the group's energies.

- Take yourself to a quite place where you will not be disturbed, and sit on a comfortable chair.
- Remove your shoes and place your feet flat on the floor. Sit as upright as is comfortable, and position your head so that you are looking straight ahead. Rest your hands on your lap with your palms up.
- Close your eyes and focus on your breathing, be aware of it drawing in and being exhaled from deep within you. To begin with, do not control your breathing but be aware of it: in… out… in… out.
- Now begin to control your breathing. Inhale for a count of four, hold for a count of four, and exhale for a count of four. Repeat this until you feel deeply relaxed and ready to begin the meditation.
- Become aware of your feet and feel the floor beneath them. Become aware of roots growing down from your feet into the earth. It does not matter how many floors up you are— just be aware of becoming a part of the earth.
- Mentally feel a flow of warm energy and light flowing up through the roots into your feet. Become aware of this wonderful warm energy and light as it slowly flows up through your ankles, then your calves and knees, and feel it inside your stomach.
- Feel the energy and light begin to slowly fill your body, smoothly, gently. When it reaches the tips of your fingers feel it flow onwards, beyond your physical body. Become aware of this warm, tingling sensation.
- Feel the cosmic energy flow through your abdomen, your throat, your head, the center of your forehead, and now up through your crown.

- You are now an open channel to the spiritual healing energy of the cosmos and the divine. Feel it as it flows through from the soles of your feet, your whole body, and onward through your crown, ever onward back to the cosmos.
- Now bathe in this wonderful feeling. If you feel a blockage anywhere, mentally direct the flow of energy to release it.
- When you feel ready, ask this healing energy to help you overcome any personal problems.
- When you are ready, direct this healing energy to help others. See the person you want to help in your mind's eye. Say their name mentally or out loud. If you cannot think of anyone in particular, send out the energy to help heal mankind and the world. (If working in a group, members should call out the names of people they particularly want helped.)
- Relax and enjoy the infusion of your soul and the cosmos until you are ready to come out of the meditative state.
- In order to come out of this meditation correctly, it is very important to "close down" correctly, or you will remain "open" and may find that you pick up a multitude of energies from those around you, or even people who pass you in the street.
- Concentrate on the rhythm of your breathing again. Inhale for a count of four, hold for a count of four, exhale for a count of four.
- Feel the warm energy and light gently drain out from the tip of your head, down through your body, draining back through the roots growing into the earth from the soles of your feet, back down into the earth.
- It is important to take a few moments for yourself before you are ready to get on with the rest of your life.

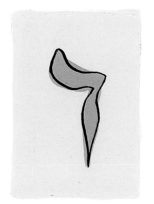 

Above: *Use candles for a wealth visualization.*

Far right: *Daled and (right), Gimel.*

Visualization to Attract Prosperity

THIS VISUALIZATION is based upon utilizing the power of the mind to achieve what you desire. In order for it to be successful, it is best performed when there is a full moon. Do not perform this visualization when there is a waning moon, because this is likely to bring a negative energy to the proceedings.

If you have them, light some candles, preferably colored green. It is a good idea to let the candles burn through to the end, although it is not completely necessary—and never leave a lit candle unattended.

• Take yourself to a quiet place, light your candles, and sit down in a comfortable chair.

• Begin your controlled breathing. Inhale for a count of four, hold for a count of four, exhale for a count of four.

• In this exercise, it is your choice whether you would prefer to keep your eyes open or shut.

• When you feel sufficiently relaxed, begin your visualization.

• Feel yourself open up spiritually to the power of the universe, and let it fill your every fiber.

• See in your mind's eye the joy that wealth and prosperity would bring to you and to your family.

• Do not at any time think about how you are going to achieve this wealth, but only the joy that it will bring.

• Dwell on these thoughts for as long as you wish.

• When you wish to come out of this visualization, concentrate on your breathing again.

• Feel the universal energy drain away from you.

• You will know when you are ready to get on with your life.

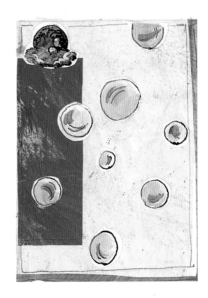

Meditation for Creativity

THIS MEDITATION WILL open you up to the creative energies of the cosmos and leave you feeling positively uplifted and full of energy. This is a good meditation to do before a busy day at home or at work, when you need to feel "buzzy" and energetic. It will open you up to the creative and inspirational worlds of Atzilut and Beriya.

Above: *A "floating" meditation inspires creativity.*

• Take yourself to a quiet place, sit on a comfortable chair, and remove your shoes.
• Close your eyes and concentrate on your breathing. Inhale for a count of four, hold for a count of four, exhale for a count of four.
• When you feel ready, begin your meditation.
• You are climbing up a flight of four stairs—count them as you go—until you reach the top, where you see an open doorway and beyond you can see a dark night glowing with a full moon and millions of bright, shining stars.
• Step through the doorway into the night, and feel the grass of a beautiful meadow under your feet.
• Take a few steps and begin to feel yourself getting lighter and lighter, until you feel that you are floating up into the stars and the galaxies.
• As you float weightlessly, you can see the earth way below, shining up at you.
• Feel the freedom and exhilaration as you float around the galaxies and open yourself up to the energy and light of the Creator.

• Enjoy the sensation as you are bathed in this wonderful energy and light as it fills every part of your being with feelings of fulfillment, energy, and self-esteem. Be proud of the person that you are, you are unique and special.
• Feel uplifted and free of any earthly worries.
• If you need help with a project, ask now for a creative input from the divine. Be open to the energy of the cosmos, and let it freely flow through you.
• Stay as long as you want floating through the cosmos until you want to return to earth.
• When you are ready, feel yourself gently floating back down until you once again feel the grass underneath your feet.
• Retrace your steps back through the door and down the four stairs.
• Concentrate on your breathing for a few moments until you feel that you are ready to get on with your life.

Meditations for Unconditional Love

KABBALAH TEACHES US that we should learn to recognize that each and every one of us is an image of the Divine, and therefore recognize the unity and holiness contained therein. These meditations will help us to learn that every person who is unconditionally loving recognizes the love and light of the Divine, present in every soul.

This meditation is written in stages so that you can either go through all of them at once, or choose the ones you wish to meditate on.

• Find a quiet place, sit on a comfortable seat, close your eyes, and relax.

• Concentrate on your breathing. Inhale and exhale deeply, feeling your stomach rise and fall. You will know when you are ready to begin.

LEARNING TO LOVE YOURSELF

• Visualize yourself sitting quietly just as you are, and begin by sending unconditional love to yourself. Do not dwell on any past mistakes—let go of any guilt, the time has come for you to get on with the rest of your life.

• Say the following words to yourself: "I am loved, I am happy, I am content with all that is in my life." Repeat this as many times as you wish. Let this remind you that you are a divine soul who deserves unconditional love. As you breathe, feel the love grow within you, repeat the words, and let them fill your heart. Take your time and feel the love grow until it fills every part of your being.

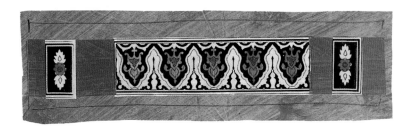

SENDING LOVE TO YOUR FAMILY, FRIENDS, AND ACQUAINTANCES

• Now imagine your family and friends as clearly as you can, and send them these same loving feelings. Most people are struggling with some form of problems, and also deserve to feel loved. Meditate on the words: "You are loved, you are happy, you are content with your life." The energy in these words will help to heal their inner feelings and will convey a feeling of love that will give them an extra lift in their lives.

SENDING LOVE TO A DIFFICULT PERSON

• Still concentrating on your breathing, imagine a person or group of people with whom you have a problem. You may even hate this person or group, but meditate on the fact that no matter what your feelings are towards this person, they too are God's creation and still deserve unconditional love.

• Mentally say the mantra while visualizing this person or group: "You are loved, you are happy, you are content with your life." You will find that by sending them this unconditional love you are actually helping yourself overcome your own resentment of them, while helping them to overcome their difficulties.

SENDING LOVE TO THE WORLD

• Continue to concentrate on your breathing, and now let the energy of love extend itself from your being to spread throughout the world. Imagine looking down onto our planet, and feel your feeling of unconditional love spread throughout.

• Repeat your mantra: "You are loved, you are happy, you are content with your life." Visualize that with every inhalation and exhalation you are filling yourself and the world up with unconditional love.

• Meditate for as long as you wish, and when you are ready, concentrate on your breathing and feel the divine energy slowly ebb out of your body. When you are ready, stand up.

Above: *Aleph.*

Meditation for Self-Confidence

KABBALAH IS FILLED with references to the mystical energies of the letter Aleph, which is the first letter of the Hebrew alphabet and therefore has the numerical value of one. It represents the one eternal God, whose energy is infinite, beyond measure. The energy contained within this letter will help you to get in touch with your egocentric inner energy, which will enhance your feelings of positive self-confidence and enable you to tap into your gifts of uniqueness and self-worth.

For this meditation, either try to visualize the letter Aleph while in your meditative state, or have a picture of it in front of you to focus on.

- Take yourself to a quiet place, sit on a comfortable chair, and relax.
- Place your feet flat on the floor, and if possible, remove your shoes.
- Close your eyes and become conscious of your breathing. Inhale for a count of four, hold for a count of four, exhale for a count of four.
- When you feel ready, either visualize Aleph or open your eyes and focus on Aleph.
- Notice the shape.
- See the three parts, the upper pointer, the lower point, and the diagonal connector.
- Concentrate on the upper pointer, and become aware that this represents the connection with your higher self, called *Nefesh Elokit*.
- Become aware that as you are breathing you are strengthening your connection with your higher self and with God.
- Now focus on the lower pointer, and become aware that this refers to your earthbound self, the *Nefesh Behamit*.

- Again, become conscious of your breathing and meditate on how these two parts co-exist within you.
- Now look at the diagonal connection that balances the two.
- Meditate on how the lower-order self, which represents ego, and the higher-order self, which represents humility and selflessness, combine to enhance your self-confidence while at the same time teaching you to use this to understand yourself better, and to help others.
- If you need help with a particular project, now is the time to ask and to be open to the answers.
- Take a moment to feel really good about yourself.
- Be open to the energies of the universe as you ask for help in understanding what a truly unique person you are, and that you have so much to offer humanity.
- When you are ready, concentrate on your breathing again and become aware of "closing down."

Above: *The Hebrew letter Hei.*

Meditation for When Things are Bad

WHEN SAID SOFTLY, the letter Hei sounds like breath. Kabbalists teach us that in order to achieve spiritual development, it is important to focus upon our breath. When meditating, it is our breathing that, with practice, leads us into achieving higher states of consciousness.

Kabbalist sages teach us that in order to fully experience the energy of the divine we must be fully alive in the present moment of our lives. The Hebrew word *heenayni*, beginning with Hei, means "Here I am" or "I am present."

When things are looking bad, reflect on the words of Rabbi Nachman of Bratslav, who declared: "Our world consists of nothing except the day and hour that we stand in now. Tomorrow is a completely different world."

• Take yourself to a quiet place, sit comfortably, and relax.

• Concentrate on your breathing. Inhale for a count of four, hold for a count of four, and exhale for a count of four.

• When you are ready, focus on the letter Hei.

• Say the letter softly, and listen as its makes the sound of breath.

• Meditate on the sound.

• Think of the miracle and beauty of breath—how it gives us the miracle of life.

• Think of God's profound act of breathing life into every creature that He has created.

• Now draw your attention back to the letter and its formation.

• Imagine yourself curled up like a ball inside the three portions of the letter. Feel safe and secure inside.

• Now notice the small gap on the top left-hand side of the letter.

• No matter how bad life seems, the divine light of God will reach you through this gap and give you love and life.

• Meditate on the fact that the light of God will always reach out to you no matter, how dark and alone you are feeling—you are never alone—God is always there for you.

• Feel the divine energy as it flows through you, giving you the strength to go forward and onward with your life—tomorrow is another day!

• When you are ready, concentrate on your breathing again as you return to your pre-meditative state.

Meditations Using The Shema

THE ANCIENT PRAYER, the Shema, expresses the fundamental teaching and focus of Kabbalah. The words are taken from the Torah (Deuteronomy 6:4), and the first line is considered by many to be the most important and powerful sentence in the Torah.

SHEMA YISRAEL, ADONAI ELOHEINU, ADONAI ECHAD

Hear/Listen O Israel, the Lord our God, the Lord is One

Below: *The Hebrew letter, Aleph.*

Top right: *Beit.*

AS A FOCUS for meditation, the Shema has little equal. The very word "*Shema*" tells the reader to hear/listen to the message contained within this one sentence with every fiber of our being. It is telling us to open up spiritually in order to experience the unity of God.

The Shema speaks to the seeker of spiritual advancement by using the address of "Israel," which is present in each and every one of those who wish to transcend our physical boundaries. The Shema tells us to listen and open up to the cosmic message of the supreme divinity of God. In order to do this correctly, we must relax and banish other thoughts from our minds completely—and the only way that this can be properly achieved is in the meditative state. You can then learn to immerse yourself into the words by learning to "feel" true meanings

The best way to use the Shema is to memorize the first sentence in the original Hebrew, because an important part of its power is in the sound and use of the words. As you will see from the following meditations based on the Shema, it is best to be able to recite it silently by memory.

ERE IS THE COMPLETE first portion of the Shema for you to read and focus on when meditating. The complete prayer is found in most Jewish prayer books.

Shema Yisrael, Ado-nai Elo-heinu, Ado-nai Echad

(Hear/Listen O Israel, the Lord our God, the Lord is one)

Baruch sheim kavod mal-chuto li-olam va-ed.

(Blessed be the name of His glorious kingdom for ever and ever.)

Vi-ahav-ta et Ado-nai Elo-hecha

(You shall love the Lord your God)

Bi-chol li-vav-cha oo-vi-chol naf-shecha oo-vi-chol mi-odecha

(With all your heart, with all your soul, and with all your might)

Vi-hayoo ha-dvarim ha-ele

(and these words which)

Asher ano-chi mi-tzavecha ha-yom al li-vavecha

(I command you this day shall be in your heart.)

Vi-shee-nantam li-vanecha vi-dee barta bam

(You shall impress them upon your children and you shall speak of them)

Bi-sheev-techa bi-vey-techa oo-vi-lech-techa va-derech

(when you sit at home and when you go on a journey)

Oo-vi-shach-bicha oo-vi-koo-mecha

(when you lie down, and when you rise up)

Ook-shartam li-hiot al ya-decha

(and you shall bind them for a sign upon your hand)

Vi-hayoo li-totafot bain ai-necha

(and they shall be as ornaments between your eyes)

Ooch-tav-tam al mi-zoo-zot bai-techa

(and you shall write them on the door-posts of your house)*

oo-vee sharecha.

(and upon your gates.)

* see Mezuzah, page 59.

Above: *Traditionally, a dead bird was swung ritually around a person to ward off worry. A contemporary interpretation is the swinging of coins in a napkin.*

Below: *The letter Lamed.*

Shema Meditation for Protection

MEDITATING ON THE SHEMA last thing at night will protect you against the forces of evil. This may sound very old-fashioned but as I touched on in Chapter 1, this is as pertinent a subject today as it has been for thousands of years.

From childhood, I have always been instinctively aware of the power of the words in the first line of the Shema, and would always recite the first line (it was the only line I knew by heart) over and over again mentally to give me protection against unseen forces, and also to stop me worrying. It is only since I have started to study and teach Kabbalah that I have discovered for myself that my intuitive instinct was right, and that Kabbalists have always taught about the protective power of the words of the Shema.

Again, as previously mentioned, the forces of evil with which we are more familiar today are jealousy, being undermined (perhaps at work), psychic attack, and bad vibes, and I am sure that if you think about it, you can easily add to the list.

I recommend to people who come to me for advice to learn and understand the first line of the Shema, and to repeat it to themselves silently before they go to sleep. In many cases people have found it even more helpful if, as well as repeating the powerful words, they are written out and placed under their pillow at night when going to sleep.

"Kabbalists have always taught about the protective power of the Shema.
Learn and understand the first line, and repeat it silently before going to sleep. The words can also be written out and placed under the pillow."

Shema Meditation for Harmony

THIS POWERFUL MEDITATION connects you to the World of Atzilut, and is in three parts. The first part will spiritually open you up to receive love, tranquility, and harmony. The second part then enables you to send out this love, harmony, and tranquility to family and friends. The third part will enable you to send love, harmony, and tranquility to the entire world.

Before beginning this meditation, it is best to try to memorize the first sentence of the Shema:

SHEMA YISRAEL, ADONAI ELOHEINU, ADONAI ECHAD
(Hear/Listen O Israel, the Lord our God, the Lord is One)

PART 1

• Take yourself to a quiet place, and sit in a comfortable seat, close your eyes, and relax.

• Place your feet flat on the floor, preferably with your shoes removed.

• Concentrate on your breathing. Inhale for a count of four, hold for a count of four, and exhale for a count of four.

• When you feel in control of your breathing, turn your attention to your feet.

• Visualize that your feet have roots growing down, deep into the earth.

• Feel as the divine energy begins to flow up through these roots, through your feet, into your body.

• Feel as it slowly begins to fill your legs, torso, and through your arms to the tips of your fingers. Be aware as it flows ever on, beyond your fingertips.

• Now feel as it flows up through your neck into your face, and up and beyond your crown.

• Visualize that this flow of energy is full of light that will connect you with the divine energy of God. Visualize the energy flowing freely beyond the crown of your head, reaching ever upward to the stars.

• Now realize yourself, your physical body, your intellect, and your emotions.

• Feel at peace with yourself.

• Enjoy the feeling as you inhale the love, harmony, and tranquility of the divine.

• Feel it as these wonderful feelings pour into every part of your being.

• Now mentally recite the Shema seven times, replacing the word "Yisrael/Israel" with your own name.

From right to left:
The letters Tet, Yod, and Kaph, mean "good," "change," and "intent."

PART 2

• Now visualize your family and friends, and send out your feelings of love, harmony, and tranquility to each and every one of them.

• Mentally recite the Shema seven times, this time replacing the word "Yisrael/Israel" with "*kehilati*/my community."

• Visualize the love and harmony of God reaching every single one of them and surrounding them with his divine light.

PART 3

• Next visualize the whole of humanity, trying to see the different cultures, religions, ages, the able, and the infirm.

• See them in your mind's eye representing the whole world as it bathes in the divine light of God.

• Now recite the Shema mentally seven times, replacing the word "Yisreal/Israel" with "*kol ha-olam*/all the world."

• Now feel the divine energy soar through you as it extends to every living creature on the earth, and then extends through to every part of the universe. See every iota of creation testifying to the greatness and unity of God.

• Now recite the Shema mentally seven times, replacing the word "Yisrael/Israel" with "*kol ha-briyah*/all of creation."

• Now let your mind flow back to the Shema in its normal wording, and begin to focus again on your breathing.

• Feel the divine energy and light slowly drain back down through every part of your body and back down into the earth.

• Take a few moments to get your bearings, and then rise and get on with the rest of your life.

Meditation for a Peaceful Night's Sleep

I AM SURE THAT YOU will have noticed that often when you wake up in the morning, your mind is still humming with your last thoughts from the previous day. People often go to bed still thinking of problems, hoping that if they "sleep on it" it will help solve those outstanding problems. This could be one of the contributory reasons why the day, according to Jewish tradition, actually begins in the evening, following the description in Genesis 1:5: "There was evening and there was morning, one day."

Kabbalist masters teach that it is important to be conscious of the presence of God both when asleep and when you wake up, and to do this successfully one should carry out the ritual *Kriyat al ha-Mitah* (the reading of the Shema upon the bed).

The following powerful meditation is based upon reading the Shema, and is complementary to *Kriyat al ha-Mitah*. It will tune you into the energy of the world of Assiya.

It is important to prepare both physically and mentally before embarking on either meditation, to make sure that you are going to have a relaxing and successful night's sleep. Take a moment to prepare yourself emotionally, letting the stress drain from your mind and body as you begin to feel calm and positive within yourself. If you have had an argument with your partner or lover during the day, always try to resolve the conflict before going to sleep—nothing should come between your thoughts of communication with God and the cosmos.

• Climb into bed, close your eyes, and focus on your breathing. Inhale for a count of four, hold for a count of four, exhale for a count of four.

• Feel your whole body relax and become aware of the flow of energy, which many feel as a warmth or slight electrical tingling, as it works its way through you from the soles of your feet, up through your legs, abdomen, chest, through the tips of your fingers, up through your throat and your head, right through to the crown of your head.

• If there is any tension or blockages, direct the energy to dissolve it.

• When you feel that your entire torso is filled up with this divine energy, turn your thoughts to God and the spiritual realms, and ask them to grant you peace and harmony during your sleeping period and when you wake up.

• Be aware that God is always with you, both during your waking and sleeping hours. Feel the divine energy bathing every part of you.

• Say aloud the following portion of the Shema:

SHEMA YISRAEL, ADONAI ELOHEINU, ADONAI ECHAD
(Hear/Listen O Israel, the Lord Our God, the Lord is One)

• Now become aware of the presence of the four angels, metaphors for the aspects of God, who will protect you when you sleep:

ABOVE YOUR HEAD
Be aware of the Shekhinah, the united presence of God, incorporating these four aspects.

BEHIND YOU
Feel the presence of Raphael, representing Netzah.
Feel the Divine healing giving you courage to endure emotional, spiritual and physical hardships.

ON YOUR LEFT
Feel the presence of Gabriel, representing Gevurah.
Feel the divine strength protecting you from your worries and fears.

ON YOUR RIGHT
Feel the presence of Michael, representing Hessed, showering you with unconditional love and forgiving your mistakes.

IN FRONT OF YOU
Feel the presence of Uriel, representing Hod.
Feel the divine light filling your soul with wisdom.

• Repeat this meditation as many times as you like, until you fall into peaceful slumber.

KABBALAH AND DREAMS

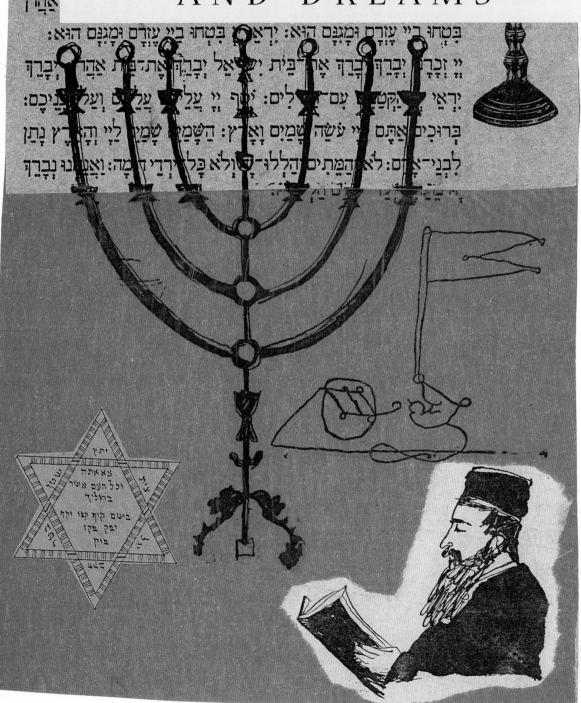

KABBALAH AND DREAMS

DREAMS ARE THE mirrors of our soul, and often convey important messages. In Kabbalah, dreams are conceived of as channels of communication with the spiritual realms.

DREAMS

In a good dream, the joy is such that (blind though I am) it all but gives me sight.

RABBI JOSEPH

There are levels upon levels within the mystery of a dream. All within the mystery of wisdom. Now come and see: Dream is one level, vision is one level, prophecy is one level. All are levels within levels, one above the other.

ZOHAR

Above: *Chet is the first letter of the "chalom," meaning "dream."*

ON THE ONE HAND our human consciousness can be invaded with dreams through which divine emissaries announce important messages, while on the other hand dreams can be induced by resorting to a variety of techniques. One only has to look at the books of the Bible to see how dreams are one of the fundamental spiritual aspects of the mystical side of Kabbalah.

By reading the accounts of Joseph's dreams in the Bible, we can see how it is fully accepted that dreams can give warnings and can foretell the

future. However, it is taught that even though a part of a dream is fulfilled, all dreams have features that are not true or part of the dream message. In Genesis 37:9–10, when Joseph recalls his dream of the sun and moon bowing down to him, "and his father said unto him, 'Shall I and thy mother indeed come?'" it should be noted that in fact his mother was already dead.

In the same vein, the view was expressed by the early Kabbalists that when you have a dream you must take your time to sort out the facts from other features: "Just as there can be no grain without straw, so there can be no dream without meaningless matter" (*Talmud*, Berachot 55a).

According to Kabbalah, there is no such thing as time on the unconscious level. All points of time, past, present, and future, all exist simultaneously. A dreamer can penetrate what we can call for simplicity the timeline at any point. This is why sometimes one can see "into the future" in dreams, when in fact we have merely unconsciously penetrated our timeline at a point further along than our present.

Dream interpretation is a fundamental aspect of Kabbalist belief. The principal biblical figure who is connected with dreams—both as a dreamer and as a dream interpreter—is Joseph. This is demonstrated in Genesis 41:13: "Each dream came true as it was interpreted to us." According to the Torah, one who knows how to interpret dreams is the true healer of the soul—and when the soul is healthy, the body will also be healthy. It continues by saying that when Joseph hears (understands) a dream to interpret it, he comprehends the light of the inner, soul dimension of the dreamer who relates his dream to him, and thereby knows how to interpret the dream.

Below: *Zayzin is a reminder of soulfulness and the need to transcend daily chores.*

Rabbi Birayim, citing a certain elder, Rabbi Banaah, said: "In Jerusalem there were twenty-four interpreters of dreams. Once I dreamed a dream and went to all of them, and not one agreed with the other in the interpretation of my dream, yet all the interpretations were fulfilled, confirming the saying, 'All dreams follow the utterances of the mouth.'"

My father totally accepted that the messages in dreams can be a warning. He had a busy confectionery shop in the West End of London. Occasionally he would dream about staff stealing cigarettes, and would always, without fail, manage to catch them with stolen cigarettes in their bags the next day—this was his own personal, foolproof alarm system.

Rabbi Hisda said, "There is reality in every dream except one that occurs during a fast. So long as a dream is not interpreted, it is like a letter that has

not been read. Neither a good dream nor a bad dream is ever entirely fulfilled. The sadness caused by a bad dream is in itself enough, and the joy caused by a good dream is in itself enough. A bad dream is worse than being flogged."

Rabbi Yochanan said, "Three kinds of dreams are fulfilled: a morning dream, a dream that a friend has about one, and a dream that is interpreted in the midst of a dream. Some say: Also a dream that is repeated."

In Kabbalist tradition a dream that is dreamed during a Friday night (Sabbath) should not be repeated until after 12 noon on the following day (Saturday), otherwise it may come true.

> **"A dream is one-sixtieth prophecy."**
> **"The unripe fruit of prophecy is a dream."**
>
> *MIDRASH*, GENESIS RABBAH 17:5

RABBIS HAVE LONG accepted that dreams can be considered a form of prophecy, but fatalism is discouraged, because impending disasters can be averted through prayer. After a bad dream the dreamer can fast, even on the Sabbath, so that the dream can be nullified. The technique for this fasting is known as *dreamfast*, and to the ancient Kabbalists it was called in Hebrew *ta'anit chalom*. It calls for fasting and self-reflection after a worrying dream.

> **"Fasting is as potent against a dream as fire is against tow [fibers**
> **of hemp]."**
>
> *TALMUD*, SHABBAT 11A

DREAMS SHOW A person's inner state, and their significance always comes to light following their interpretation.

The sages said in the name of Rabbi Yochanan: "He who has a dream and is worried about it should have it given a good meaning in the presence of

three. He should bring three (friends) and say to them, 'It is good, and may it be good. May He who is everywhere turn it to good. Seven times may it be decreed for you from heaven that it should be good,' and it will be good."

Therefore if you have a disturbing dream, the following ritual should be performed the next morning in front of three good friends. The sincere wishes of the three can bring about the dream's favorable interpretation. The dreamer does not necessarily have to tell his friends the dream, but must have it in mind during the ritual.

Above: *Gather three good friends and recite the prayer below to banish bad feelings after a disturbing dream.*

Below: *Pei (bottom) symbolizes sound and Ayin (top) vision. Talking about what we see in dreams is part of Kabbalah.*

Prayer for Ameliorating a Dream

THIS RITUAL APPEARS in some *siddurim* (prayer books) with minor variations. The text and instructions printed here are from the *Siddur Otzar HaTefillot*.

THE PASSAGES IN BOLD TYPE are recited by the dreamer; those in italics are recited by the three friends in unison.
Do not interpretations belong to God? Relate it to me, if you please.
Recite seven times: **I have seen a good dream.**
You have seen a good dream. It is good and may it become good. May the Merciful One transform it to the good. May it be decreed upon it seven times from heaven that it become good and always be good. It is good and may it become good.
The following verses speak of transformation of distress and relief.
You have changed for me my lament into dancing; you undid my sackcloth and girded me with gladness.
Then the maiden shall rejoice in a dance, and lads and elders together; and I shall change their mourning to joy, and I shall console them and gladden their sorrow. Adonai, your God, did not wish to pay heed to Balaam, and

Above: *Hands with Kabbalistic symbols.*

Below: *The letter Samekh.*

Adonai, your God, transformed for you the curse to blessing for Adonai, your God, loves you.

The following verses speak of rescue.

He redeemed my soul in peace from the battles that were upon me, for the sake of the multitudes who were with me.

And the people said to Saul, "Shall Jonathan die, who performed this great salvation for Israel? A sacrilege!"—as Adonai lives, if a hair of his head falls to the ground, for with Adonai has he acted this day! "And the people redeemed Jonathan, and he did not die. Those redeemed by God will return and arrive at Zion with glad song and eternal gladness on their heads; joy and gladness shall they attain, and sorrow and groan shall flee."

The following verses speak of peace.

I create fruit of the lips: "Peace, peace, for far and near," says Adonai, "and I shall heal him."

A spirit clothed Amasai, head of the officers, "For your sake, David, and to be with you, son of Jesse; peace to you, and peace to him who helps you, for your God has helped you." David accepted them and appointed them heads of the band. And you shall say: "So may it be as long as you live; peace for you, peace for your household and peace for all that is with you. Adonai will give might to His people, Adonai will bless His people with peace."

The following verses are recited three times each:

Adonai, I heard what you made me hear and I was frightened.

Adonai, during these years, give him life, Adonai, during these years, make it known: amid rage remember to be merciful.

A song to ascents, I raise my eyes to the mountains: whence will

come my help? My help is from Adonai, Maker of heaven and earth.

He will not allow your foot to falter; your Guardian will not slumber. Behold, He neither slumbers nor sleeps—the Guardian of Israel. Adonai is your Guardian; Adonai is your Shade at your right hand. By day the sun will not harm you, nor the moon by night. Adonai will protect you from every evil; He will guard your soul. Adonai will guard your departure and your arrival, from this time and forever.

Adonai spoke to Moses, saying: Speak to Aaron and his sons, saying: So are you to bless the Children of Israel, say to them:

May Adonai bless you and safeguard you. May Adonai illuminate His countenance for you and be gracious to you. May Adonai turn His countenance to you and establish peace for you. Let them place My name upon the Children of Israel, and I will bless them.

May You reveal to me the path of life.

The fullness of joys in Your Presence; there is a delight at your right hand for eternity.

Recite once: *Go with joy, eat your bread and drink your wine with a glad heart, for God has already approved your deeds. And repentance, prayer, and charity remove the evil of the decrees. And peace be upon us and upon all Israel. Amen.*

IT WAS CONSIDERED a bad sign for someone not to dream for a continuous period of seven days. Rabbi Ze'era said: "A man who goes seven days without a dream is called evil, for Scripture says, 'He that hath it shall abide satisfied; he shall not be visited with evil.'" It was also very bad to see certain things in a dream, such as being given a present by a dead person.

In their dreams Kabbalists would make heavenly journeys, and some mystics would claim to receive the answers to their enquiries which had been made to God. Through Kabbalah we learn that God reaches out to us through dreams, bringing us guidance while at the same time refreshing and nourishing our spirits. We need to confront our dreams honestly, rather than ignoring them, and should take heed of the messages contained in our dreams, realizing that they may be a warning that we may have to take a certain action.

The technique of "dream questions" is derived from a neglected realm of Kabbalah called *she'elot chalom*, i.e. questions formulated before going to sleep whose answers were expected to arrive in dreams. In many cases the answers took the form of a biblical verse that was somehow related to the question, which had to be interpreted in its turn. There are many examples of *she'elot chalom* in ancient Kabbalistic manuscripts.

Rabbi Chaim Vital recommended, "You shall go to bed to sleep, pray 'Let it be Your Will,' and use one of the pronunciations of the [divine] names written in front of you and direct your thought to which of the mystical

Above: *Weeping has been thought to induce a dream-like state that brings prophetic visions.*

spheres it is related. Then mention your question either to discover issues related to a dream and future things, or to achieve whatever thing you wish and afterwards ask [the question]."

The following Kabbalist exercise can be performed if you are looking for an answer to a problem or for personal guidance. Before going to bed, write down your question, and meditate on it for several minutes before placing it under your pillow. Ask your dream self for an answer. A vivid dream should invariably follow, which offers a helpful answer to your question. This particular method is practiced in many cultures throughout the world, and is often referred to as *dream incubation*.

Another dream-inducing Kabbalist technique is that of *mystical weeping*. The theory behind this is that as the direct result of self-induced weeping one can acquire a paranormal consciousness or vision containing important information. Likewise in apocalyptic literature there are many examples where praying, fasting, and weeping are used to induce the Word of God in a dream.

FROM THE SAME Kabbalist school of thought came the technique of *color visualization* to attain answers to questions, to be received in a state similar to that when dreaming. Kabbalists would visualize various colors upon which certain letters would be written:

> **And you should imagine in your thought that you ask your question from those combinations of letters written there, and they will answer your question, or they will dwell their spirit in your mouth, or you will be drowsy and they will answer you, like in a dream.**
>
> PROFESSOR MOSHE IDEL

THESE DREAM TECHNIQUES—dream questions, color visualization, mystical weeping—are an important mystical aspect of Kabbalah. They give credence to the belief that the Kabbalist can take the initiative in establishing contact with the spiritual realms, and that particular experiences can be achieved by resorting to these specific techniques.

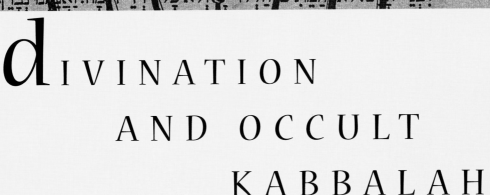

יֹאמְרוּ הַגּוֹיִם אַיֵּה־נָא אֱלֹהֵיהֶם: וֵאלֹהֵינוּ בַשָּׁמָיִם כֹּל אֲשֶׁר־חָפֵץ
עָשָׂה: עֲצַבֵּיהֶם כֶּסֶף וְזָהָב מַעֲשֵׂה יְדֵי אָדָם: פֶּה־לָהֶם וְלֹא יְדַבֵּרוּ עֵינַיִם
לָהֶם וְלֹא יִרְאוּ: אָזְנַיִם לָהֶם וְלֹא יִשְׁמָעוּ אַף לָהֶם וְלֹא יְרִיחוּן: יְדֵיהֶם
וְלֹא יְמִישׁוּן רַגְלֵיהֶם וְלֹא יְהַלֵּכוּ לֹא־יֶהְגּוּ בִּגְרוֹנָם: כְּמוֹהֶם יִהְיוּ עֹשֵׂיהֶם
כֹּל אֲשֶׁר־בֹּטֵחַ בָּהֶם: יִשְׂרָאֵל בְּטַח בַּיָי עֶזְרָם וּמָגִנָּם הוּא: בֵּית אַהֲרֹן
בִּטְחוּ בַיָי עֶזְרָם וּמָגִנָּם הוּא: יִרְאֵי יְיָ בִּטְחוּ בַיָי עֶזְרָם וּמָגִנָּם הוּא:
יְיָ זְכָרָנוּ יְבָרֵךְ יְבָרֵךְ אֶת־בֵּית יִשְׂרָאֵל יְבָרֵךְ אֶת־בֵּית אַהֲרֹן: יְבָרֵךְ
יִרְאֵי יְיָ הַקְּטַנִּים עִם־הַגְּדֹלִים: יֹסֵף יְיָ עֲלֵיכֶם עֲלֵיכֶם וְעַל־בְּנֵיכֶם:
בְּרוּכִים אַתֶּם לַיָי עֹשֵׂה שָׁמַיִם וָאָרֶץ: הַשָּׁמַיִם שָׁמַיִם לַיָי וְהָאָרֶץ נָתַן
לִבְנֵי־אָדָם: לֹא הַמֵּתִים יְהַלְלוּ־יָהּ וְלֹא כָּל־יֹרְדֵי דוּמָה: וַאֲנַחְנוּ נְבָרֵךְ

dIVINATION
AND OCCULT
KABBALAH

dIVINATION AND OCCULT KABBALAH

DIVINATION

DIVINATION IS THE TERM widely used to cover a variety of means of predicting the future. Although rabbis frown upon the use of divination, one must ask whether there is much difference between the spontaneous prophecies of the prophets and those of psychics who have a special gift.

THE PRIMARY OBJECTIVE of Kabbalah is to achieve spirituality and thus begin to live fully, using all of our six senses. Within our understanding of this expanded world we can begin to appreciate the wonders of psychic phenomena. As we begin to understand the mystical teachings contained within Kabbalah, so we can begin to appreciate that there is much within our unconscious levels that we do not and cannot understand—it is beyond logic and reason. Therefore we should also take on board that there are certain gifted people who are tuned into certain unconscious levels of our existence, who can, with the aid of divination tools such as cards, charting the stars, reading palms, and crystal-gazing, see the future.

The main principle behind divination that is upheld in Kabbalah is that time is an extension as well as an expression of mind. All time is

simultaneous, and the past, present, and future can be viewed at any time by those who have the gift. This is along the lines of Kabbalist teaching that whatever is done at any point in time has an impact on another point in the time line, sometimes in the future, but just as easily in the past.

To better understand these teachings, picture a book and flip through the pages of the beginning, middle, and end. In actual fact, you can open up any page you wish to view the contents—so it is with life. This example makes it easier to understand that past, present, and future are all open to the unconscious levels to view. Divination is the tool by which we can unlock these unconscious levels.

Below: *The letter Tav.*
Opposite (top): *Nun.*
Opposite (below): *Mem.*

Kabbalah and the Tarot

TAROT IS PERHAPS one of the best known methods of divination that uses symbols to trigger meanings embedded in our subconscious minds. The make-up of a Tarot pack can be seen as a symbolic representation of Kabbalah. Each deck consists of seventy-eight cards divided into two groups, the Major Arcana and the Minor Arcana. It was the nineteenth-century French Rosicrucian and Kabbalist, Eliphas Levi, who stressed the link between the twenty-two letters of the Hebrew alphabet and the twenty-two cards that form the Major Arcana. By this virtue, they are also seen as relating to the twenty-two paths on the Tree of Life and the stages of evolution. There is no evidence for any connection between the Tree of Life and the Tarot deck before the late eighteenth century.

The following connections are based on those as laid down by the Golden Dawn, and are the most commonly used in the English-speaking world.

THE MAJOR ARCANA AND THE TWENTY-TWO PATHS

Above: *The letter Aleph, which relates to The Fool in the Major Arcana of the Tarot.*

AS CAN BE SEEN in the chart below and opposite, the twenty-two cards of the Major Arcana represent the twenty-two paths that connect the Minor Arcana. Each path signifies the interaction between the pair of Sephirot that it connects.

The Major Arcana are very powerful images that have a triple aspect: symbolical, numerical (and alphabetical), and astrological. Each Hebrew letter is also a corresponding number.

KABBALAH AND THE MAJOR ARCANA

LETTER	PATH	CARD	TRUMP	ASTROLOGICAL TAROT
1. ALEPH	11	FOOL	0	URANUS
2. BEIT	12	MAGICIAN	1	MERCURY
3. GIMEL	13	PRIESTESS	2	MOON
4. DALED	14	EMPRESS	3	VENUS
5. HEI	15	EMPEROR	4	MARS
6. VOV	16	HIEROPHANT	5	VENUS
7. ZAYIN	17	LOVERS	6	MERCURY
8. CHET	18	CHARIOT	7	MOON
9. TET	19	STRENGTH	8	SUN
10. YOD	20	HERMIT	9	MERCURY
11. KAPH	21	WHEEL	10	JUPITER
12. LAMED	22	JUSTICE	11	VENUS
13. MEM	23	HANGED MAN	12	NEPTUNE
14. NUN	24	DEATH	13	MARS
15. SAMEKH	25	TEMPERANCE	14	JUPITER
16. AYIN	26	DEVIL	15	SATURN
17. PEI	27	TOWER	16	MARS
18. TZADDI	28	STAR	17	URANUS/SATURN
19. KUF	29	THE MOON	18	MOON
20. RESH	30	THE SUN	19	SUN
21. SHIN	31	JUDGMENT	20	PLUTO
22. TAV	32	THE WORLD	21	SATURN

MEANING	ELEMENT	COLOR OF PATH – QUEEN SCALE
OBSESSION	AIR	SKY BLUE
CREATIVITY	AIR	PURPLE
WISDOM	WATER	SILVER
ATTAINMENT	EARTH	MID BLUE
AUTHORITY	FIRE	LIGHT BLUE
KINDNESS	EARTH	INDIGO
LOVE/HARMONY	AIR	MAUVE
CHOICES/ADVERSITY	WATER	MAROON
COURAGE/CONVICTION	AIR	DEEP PURPLE
PRUDENCE	AIR	SLATE GRAY
DESTINY	WATER	DARK BLUE
FAIRNESS/BALANCE	AIR	BLUE
INTUITION/TRANSITION	WATER	SEA GREEN
SUDDEN CHANGE	FIRE	BROWN
PATIENCE	FIRE	YELLOW
BONDAGE	EARTH	BLACK
CHAOS	FIRE	BRIGHT RED
HOPE	AIR	RED
HIDDEN PROBLEMS	WATER	BUFF
HAPPINESS/SUCCESS	AIR/FIRE	GOLDEN YELLOW
RENEWAL	FIRE	VERMILLION
GREAT SUCCESS	EARTH	BLACK

THE MAJOR ARCANA AND THE TREE OF LIFE

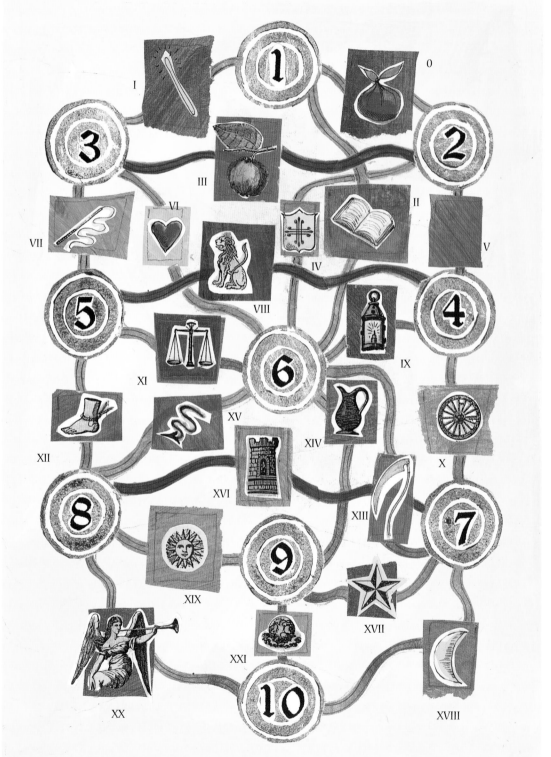

KEY 0 Fool; I Magician; II High Priestess; III Express; IV Emperor; V Hierophant; VI Lovers; VII Chariot; VIII Strength; IX Hermit; X Wheel of Fortune; XI Justice; XII Hanged Man; XIII Death; XIV Temperance; XV Devil; XVI Tower; XVII Star; XVIII Moon; XIX Sun; XX Judgement; XXI World

Above: *The letter Resh is linked to the Major Arcana card The Sun in the Tarot deck.*

SINCE ANCIENT TIMES scholars have known that it is much easier to acquire and retain large tracts of knowledge when it is related to images, rather than just in words and numbers. This is one of the underlying principles of the images of the Tarot deck. Experienced Tarot readers form strong memory links between the concepts of the Major Arcana and the letters and paths of the Tree of Life.

The following are some of the images associated with each of the ten Sephirot on the Tree of Life, which can be of use when reading Tarot. These images can be seen in many early artistic works illustrating the Tree of Life, and are used by those following the Western Mystery Tradition of Kabbalist teaching.

KETER	BEARDED MAN SEEN IN PROFILE, FACE SEEN IN PROFILE
HOKHMAH	BEARDED MAN, FACE FULL-ON
BINAH	MATURE WOMAN ON THRONE
HESSED	MIGHTY KING
GEVURAH	MIGHTY WARRIOR, WARRIOR QUEEN
TIFERET	KING, CHILD, SACRIFICED GOD
NETZAH	BEAUTIFUL NAKED WOMAN
HOD	WINGED MERCURY, HERMES OR HERMAPHRODITE
YESOD	STRONG AND POWERFUL MAN
MALKHUT	YOUNG WOMAN ON A THRONE, BRIDE IN FINERY

THE MINOR ARCANA AND THE SEPHIROT

THE TEN NUMBERED cards in each of the four suits of the Minor Arcana correspond to the ten Sephirot. Put simply, all the fives in any suite would correspond with the fifth Sephirot, Gevurah. Just as the Sephirot follow a sequence from the first point of creation in the first Sephirah (Keter) through to the completion in the tenth (Malkhut), so the numbered cards follow this same pattern, from the ones or aces through to the tens.

AS WE HAVE SEEN, Kabbalists view the Tree of Life as developing through the Four Worlds, Atzilut, Beriya, Yetzira, and Assiya. In Tarot you will find that each of the four suits of the Minor Arcana also corresponds to one of the Four Worlds. The following chart gives you a simplified example of this, together with the corresponding elements:

TAROT SUIT	ELEMENT	KABBALIST WORLD
PENTACLES	EARTH	ASSIYA (MANIFEST WORLD)
SWORDS	AIR	YETZIRA (FORMATIVE WORLD)
CUPS	WATER	BERIYA (CREATIVE WORLD)
WANDS	FIRE	ATZILUT (ARCHETYPAL WORLD)

Eliphas Levy also connected the four suits of the Minor Arcana with the letters forming the unpronounceable name of God, called the Tetragrammaton, which is represented by **YHVH:**

Y	**WANDS**	**FIRE**
H	**CUPS**	**WATER**
V	**SWORDS**	**AIR**
H	**PENTACLES**	**EARTH**

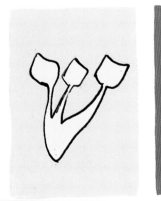  

OCCULT KABBALAH

WHEN THE KNOWLEDGE learned in practical Kabbalah is used as a basis for rituals in order to produce a physical manifestation, this becomes known as Occult Kabbalah.

Many traditional Kabbalists object to magic, saying that it can alter the balance of the Tree of Life and therefore disturb the proper order and balance of nature. It is also said that a magician can become so engrossed in the properties in the World of Yetzira that he cannot enter the Worlds above. To many, especially rabbis, the use of sacred names is considered blasphemous, and yet many people practice Kabbalistic magic with good intentions and within the spirit of submission to God.

The modern form of magic, often referred to as Western Magic, became popular when the leaders of the Golden Dawn movement developed the correlation between the twenty-two letters of the Hebrew Alphabet with the twenty-two pathways of the Tree of Life, and also with the Tarot.

THE PATHWAYS OR CHANNELS of the Tree of Life are used to facilitate higher states of consciousness by meditation and visualization. Followers of the Golden Dawn called this "scrying in the spirit vision" and "rising on the planes." The most important purpose of the Tree of Life is to produce a framework for understanding the natures of the macrocosm (universe) and microcosm (mankind).

In order to incorporate Kabbalah into Western Magic, devotees learn how to read and understand the power within the Hebrew letters (see page 148), their meanings, divine names, associations with the Tree of Life, astrology, and the Tarot.

Above: *Many practitioners of western magic study Kabblah, astrology, Tarot, and the study of Hebrew letters.*

Opposite: *(From right), the letters Vav, Kuf, and Shin.*

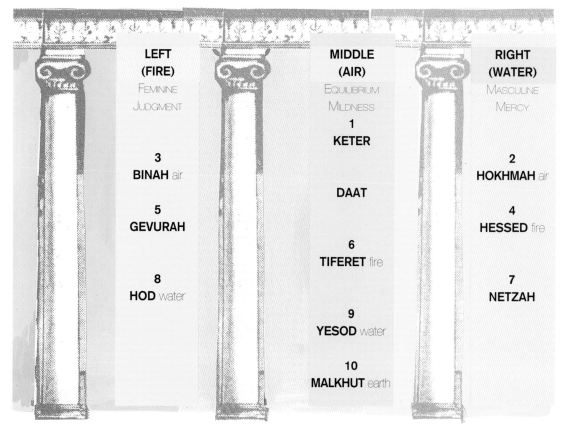

LEFT (FIRE)	MIDDLE (AIR)	RIGHT (WATER)
FEMININE JUDGMENT	EQUILIBRIUM MILDNESS	MASCULINE MERCY
	1 KETER	
3 BINAH air		2 HOKHMAH air
	DAAT	
5 GEVURAH		4 HESSED fire
	6 TIFERET fire	
8 HOD water		7 NETZAH
	9 YESOD water	
	10 MALKHUT earth	

Above: *The Sephirot of the Tree of Life depicted on three pillars shows how the left and right (feminine and masculine) Sephirot work in pairs, with the central column acting as mediator.*

Below: *The letter Hei.*

One of the basic principles of magic using the Tree of Life is balance, and therefore the understanding that the Sephirot work in pairs with their power synthesized through the Sephirot of the middle column. This is a vital ingredient to any magic done when using the Tree of Life, because if all of the energies are used on only one of the Sephirot on either the left- or right-hand column, then the power of the whole Tree could be thrown out of balance, and any physical manifestation could be of a negative type.

The Sephirot situated within the left-hand pillar represent the female-negative-passive principle, and those within the right-hand pillar represent the male-positive-active principle. Those situated within the middle pillar represent equilibrium and harmony, and are the balancing factor between the Sephirot of the other two Pillars.

Magicians recognize that each of the Sephirot is ruled by one of the sacred names of God, and therefore they perceive that they are also representatives of nature. It is therefore recognized that the Tree of Life can be looked at in relation to the elements. The illustration above shows the two elements associated with each sephirot. For example, the sphere of Binah is a combination of fire (like all the sephirot of the left column) and air, and would be known as Fire of Air; Yesod would be known as Air of Water. Sephirot without elements next to them have both elements the same.

F ROM THIS CHART we can understand why the Star of David is such a powerful symbol, because its shape demonstrates the balance and dependency between the right-hand pillar—water—with the left—fire—harmonizing them with the middle pillar.

In most magical rituals, names and words are an important ingredient. When a magician is in training, he learns to build up a magical alphabet, vocabulary, and language through which he can communicate with the universe what his intentions are when he is performing spells. They are also used by the magician to help learn from the universe.

The ten Sephirot that comprise the Tree of Life can be likened to an enormous filing system or database. There are numerous systems of correspondences that can be linked to each of the Sephirot. The Kabbalist, therefore, by working with the specific energy contained within each of the spheres, can use it to help him to carry out his work.

There are many lists of these "magical correspondences" that help translate language into an orderliness of thought that relates and transforms perception into other lines of thought and awareness. They are symbols that help to explain reality, they are not reality itself. They can also be used to create links with the Tree of Life in order to create magical talismans and seals. Some are listed within the Tarot section, and here are some more examples used in modern magic:

Above (left): *the Star of David; (right), stars of David in a book traditionally thought to have been given to Adam by the archangel Raziel.*
Below: *The Hebrew letter Daled.*

131

NATURE AND THE TREE OF LIFE

SEPHIROT	PLANT OR TREE	GEMS	ANIMALS
1. KETER	ALMOND TREE	DIAMOND	SWAN
2. HOKHMAH	MISTLETOE	TURQUOISE	EAGLE
3. BINAH	CYPRESS	STAR SAPPHIRE	BEE
4. HESSED	OLIVE TREE	LAPIS LAZULI	UNICORN
5. GEVURAH	OAK, HICKORY	RUBY	WOLF
6. TIFERET	OAK, ACORN	TOPAZ	LION
7. NETZAH	LAUREL, MYRTLE	EMERALD	RAVEN, DOVE
8. HOD	PALM TREE	OPAL	JACKAL
9. YESOD	GINSENG	QUARTZ	DOG, ELEPHANT
10. MALKHUT	IVY, WHEAT, WILLOW	ROCK CRYSTAL	BULL, SPHINX

PLEASE NOTE THAT THIS IS NOT A COMPLETE TABLE AND IS ONLY AN EXAMPLE OF SOME OF THE MAGICAL CORRESPONDENCES OF THE TREE OF LIFE IN NATURE. FOR FURTHER INFORMATION THE READER IS DIRECTED TO THE WORK BY ALEISTER CROWLEY, ENTITLED *777.*

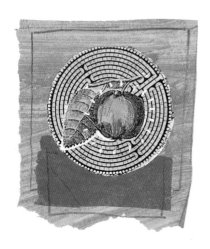

SEPHIROT	PLANET	PHYSICAL CORRESPONDENCES	MAGICAL IMAGES
1. KETER	FIRST SWIRLINGS	CROWN	BEARDED KING PROFILE
2. HOKHMAH	ZODIAC	LEFT SIDE OF FACE	BEARDED KING FULL FACE
3. BINAH	SATURN	RIGHT SIDE OF FACE	MATRON
4. HESSED	JUPITER	LEFT ARM	CROWNED AND THRONED KING
5. GEVURAH	MARS	RIGHT ARM	WARRIOR IN CHARIOT
6. TIFERET	SUN	BREAST	CHILD, KING
7. NETZAH	VENUS	LEGS, HIPS, LOINS	BEAUTIFUL NAKED WOMAN
8. HOD	MERCURY	LEGS, LOINS	HERMAPHRODITE
9. YESOD	MOON	REPRODUCTIVE ORGANS	BEAUTIFUL NAKED MAN
10. MALKHUT	EARTH FOR ELEMENTS	ANUS, FEET	YOUNG FEMALE THRONED AND CROWNED

FLOWERS AND FRUITS

ALMOND FLOWER
AMARANTH
LILY
FOUR-LEAFED CLOVER
NETTLE
SUNFLOWER
ROSE, FIG, APPLE
LIME
GARDENIA, ORCHID
POMEGRANATE

MAGICAL CORRESPONDENCES
AND THE TREE OF LIFE

SYMBOLS	VIRTUES	VICE
POINT	ATTAINMENT	NONE
PHALLUS, STRAIGHT LINE	DEVOTION	NONE
CUP, FEMALE SEX ORGANS	SILENCE	AVARICE
TETRAHEDRON, ORB	OBEDIENCE, GENEROSITY	GLUTTONY, BIGOTRY, TYRANNY, HYPOCRISY
SWORD PENTAGON	COURAGE	DESTRUCTION, TYRANNY, VENGEANCE
CUBE	DEVOTION	PRIDE
LAMP, ROSE	UNSELFISHNESS	LUST, UNCHASTITY
APRON	TRUTHFULNESS	DISHONESTY
PERFUME	INDEPENDENCE	IDLENESS
EQUAL-ARMED CROSS	DISCRIMINATION	INERTIA

Kabbalah and the Magical Powers of the Moon

The sun shall not smite thee by day, nor the moon by night.

PSALMS 121:6

Above: *The letter Gimel.*
Below: *The letter Beit.*

THE MOON IS UNIVERSALLY believed to exert a powerful influence upon our lives. Throughout the ages, Kabbalists and the general Jewish population have rarely embarked on important activities without having first taken into account phases of the moon. In common with anyone with a working knowledge of magic, they were well aware that the waxing moon stimulates growth and development, the waning moon promotes decay, and the full moon is the time of its full power. This is illustrated in the following prayer, which is still used today to stop the moon from waning:

May it be Your will, Adonai, my God and the God of my forefathers, to fill the flaw of the moon that there be no diminution in it. May the light of the moon be like the light of sun and like the light of the seven days of creation as it was before it was diminished, as it is said, "The two great luminaries." And may there be fulfilled upon us the verse that is written: They shall seek Adonai, their God, and David their King. Amen.

THE KABBALIST ELEAZER of Worms, Germany, warned his followers that trees should not be cut down, grains and fruit should not be harvested, or clothes soaked in water while the moon is waning, because they would quickly rot away. He also is said to have diagnosed that some mental ailments were due to the moon's effects on the brain.

One should not cut one's fingernails or hair on the day of the new moon. This relates to the belief that one should not bring attention to any kind of growth during this period, because this could lead to bad luck.

The period of the waxing moon is the best time to celebrate a marriage, because it is said that it will bring good luck. If one conceives during this

time, it is considered especially favorable for the child, and this is the best time to move into a new home.

The day of the new moon is the best time to begin a new business, to begin a new study course, and in times gone past, this was the best time for a child to begin school.

Above: *Kabbalists acknowledge the influence of the moon's phases.*

SANCTIFICATION OF THE MOON/KIDDUSH LEVANAH

THE SANCTIFICATION of the Moon is a ritual that was created during Talmudic times and is still practiced today. One reason for this is that Rabbi Yochana taught that one who blesses the new moon during the correct period is regarded as one who is greeting the Shekinah—God's presence. By watching and being aware of the different phases of the moon, we are seeing a tiny part of the miracle of God's creation.

The other reason is that because of its monthly reappearance, the phases of the moon can be equated with the history of the Jews and

Above: *(From right) The letters Kaph, Lamed, and Aleph.*

therefore Kabbalah. Just as the moon is reborn after a period of decline, so the Jewish people and their teachings regularly reappear after going through periods of decline and persecution.

The new-moon blessing should customarily be said in the open air when the new moon is visible, between the fourth and sixteenth of the month. It should not be recited on the Sabbath, unless it is the last remaining night before the mid-month deadline.

Hallelujah! Praise Adonai from the heavens; praise Him in the heights. Praise Him, all His angels; praise Him, all His legions. Praise Him, sun and moon; praise Him, all bright stars. Praise Him, the most exalted of the heavens and the waters that are above the heavens. Let them praise the Name of Adonai, for He commanded and they were created. And He established them forever and ever, He issued a decree that will not change.

One should look at the moon before reciting this blessing:

Blessed are You, Adonai, our God, King of the Universe, Who with His utterance created the heavens, and with the breath of His mouth all their legion. A decree and a schedule did He give them that they not alter their assigned task. They are joyous and glad to perform the will of their Owner—the Worker of truth Whose work is truth. To the moon He said that it should renew itself as a crown of splendor for those borne (by Him) from the womb, those who are destined to renew themselves like it, and to glorify their Molder for the name of His glorious kingdom, Blessed are You, Adonai, Who renews the months.

SOME OF THE PRACTICES that relate to this rite include one first mentioned in a work composed in the post-Talmudic period, called the *Masekhet Soferim*, which refers to the practice of skipping three times at the close of

the blessing and addressing the moon three times, saying, "As I skip before you and do not reach you, so, if others jump before me may they not strike me," and then three times saying to your neighbor, "Peace be unto you."

In Medieval times threefold repetitions were commonly associated with various forms of magic. After performing the above, it was the practice to shake one's clothes to "cast off the spirits." Anyone practicing the full rite was thought to have protection from death during the following month.

Traditionally, the new lunar month is celebrated by the festival of the New Moon—Rosh Hodesh. During the previous Sabbath ceremony, the date of the new moon is announced, and the shofar (ram's horn) is blown as the congregation prays to God to make it a successful and joyous new month. The one exception to this is the Sabbath preceding the month of Tishri, when Rosh Hashanah (Jewish New Year) occurs. The shofar is not blown in order to fool the Angel of Death, who enjoys causing chaos with people's lives during the festivities of the New Year.

During the Sabbath ceremony, when the date of the new moon is announced, the congregation prays to God to make the new month one of blessing and joy. In ancient times, this date was determined by the Rabbinic Court. Today there is no problem in setting the date, and the beginning of the Jewish month (which is different to the one used in the rest of the world in that it is lunar, and it is dated from the beginning of time) occurs when the moon is exactly between the sun and the Earth, and is therefore rendered invisible. This is the point at which the birth of the moon takes place, called in Hebrew the *molad*.

In the sixteenth-century center for Kabbalistic study in Safed, the custom, still in practice today, of fasting on the eve of the new moon was established. This arose because the Kabbalists saw the waning of the moon as a symbol of the absence of God's presence from the world, and the disintegration of humanity. The next day is treated as a feast day, a symbol of hope and renewal.

ROSH HODESH
'THE FESTIVAL OF THE NEW MOON'

The Legend of the Golem

It is said in the name of Rabbi Eleazar: As the Lord was creating Adam, He had come to the stage when Adam had the form of a golem, an unarticulated lump, which lay prone from one end of the world to the other. With regard to this, Scripture says: Thine eyes did see my unformed substance (golem).

I N THE QUOTE ABOVE, Adam is described as a golem during the period of his formation, but before God blows life and even more importantly, a soul, into him.

Stories of artificial creations conjured up by Kabbalists began to appear during the Talmudic period (before 500 CE). The creation of a golem by Rabbi Abba ben Rav Hamma (Rav) is recorded in the Talmud during this period (fourth century CE):

Rav created a man. He sent it before Rav Zera. He spoke to it, but it did not answer. He said, "You must have been created by one of my colleagues. Return to dust."

TALMUD, SANHEDRIN 65B

T O THE WRITERS of the Talmud, the creation of a golem was not considered a particularly remarkable feat. The power of the written word, alchemy and the names of God were well-known to these early Kabbalists, and their study of the *Sepher Yetzirah* was the ideal framework for making the creation of a golem feasible. It is believed that many holy rabbis and sages were able to create human and animal golems, such as Rabbis Khanaina and Hoshaya, who, through their meditations, created a third-grown calf which they slaughtered and ate just before each Sabbath.

The legend of the Golem is one of the most fascinating aspects of the use of the magical elements of Kabbalah. Not only have various legends

about golems been passed down orally, but they have also been a well-known literary subject since the nineteenth century, within both Jewish and non-Jewish circles.

The twentieth century saw this interest grow, with writers using the legend to reflect their contemporary conditions, and also by using it as the basis of science fiction. There have also been a number of films made on the subject of golems, such as two separate versions of *Der Golem* (1914 and 1920), and as diverse as *The Golem and the Dancer* (1917) and a golem film set in the twenty-ninth century. The golem has also appeared in the TV program *The X Files*, and there are hundreds of websites dedicated to the legend, as well as numerous books.

Many writers see the link between the golem and Mary Shelley's monster, Victor Frankenstein. In 1808, eight years before *Frankenstein* was written, Jacob Grimm (co-author of *Kinder-und Hausmärchen*, *Grimm's Fairy Tales*) had written about the remarkable golem legend. Mary Shelley's introduction to her story mentions that she had spent a part of the summer of 1816 in Geneva reading German ghost stories.

In order to understand the background of the golem legends it is important to understand the ritual bloodthirsty murder of Jews called the "Blood Libel," which occurred throughout Europe over many hundreds of years. The basis of the libel was that Jews killed Christian children for sacrificial means, especially on Passover, when it was said that the child's blood was mixed with the ingredients of the matzo which is eaten during this festival. This libel was often invoked if a Christian child was missing; its dead or murdered body would be planted in a Jewish house, often by a priest, who would then "discover" the body and lead a mob on a murderous rampage through the ghetto. This would then be an excuse for the Church to confiscate a large amount of Jewish property. Jews were also supposed to desecrate the holy wafers. This anti-Semitic folklore has been the cause of the deaths of hundreds, if not thousands of innocent Jewish men, women, and children.

Many legends have been handed down through the years about golems. The most famous, however, is the legend of the Golem of Prague.

Opposite: *The letter Yod.*
Below: *Chet (bottom) and Tet (top).*

THE GOLEM OF PRAGUE

RABBI JUDAH LOEW BEN BAZALEL (*c.*1525–1609) was known as the Maharal of Prague. He was a Talmudist, Kabbalist moralist, astronomer, and mathematician, and was appointed Chief Rabbi of Prague *c.*1571 at a time of great oppression to the Jews because of the Blood Libel.

In 1580, he asked a question in his dreams as to how he could oppose the Christian priests who fuelled this charge. The answer was a combination of letters of the Hebrew alphabet, which the sage realized contained the various combinations of the names of the divine. And he realized that by using this permutation he could form a living golem from the earth. Therefore, together with his son-in-law and a disciple, he set to work to create a living Golem.

In order for this creation to take place he had to invoke the forces of the four elements—air, water, fire, and earth. He was born under the element of air, his son-in-law was born under the element of fire, and his disciple was born under the element of water. Therefore, between them, they could not bring the work of creation to completion until they had gone to the riverbank and found an area containing clay and mud, the element of earth, and there they fashioned the shape of a man.

The Golem was brought to life by enacting a magical ritual and by putting a piece of paper on which were written the magical and life-creating letters—SH-E-M—the ineffable Name of God, into his mouth. He had no power of speech and completely obeyed the Rabbi. He would act as a servant, drawing water, chopping wood, etc., but was only able to obey exact orders, and one legend, which may have been the inspiration for *The Sorcerer's Apprentice*, is that when the Golem was told to fetch water he was not told how much, and a minor flood occurred.

At night the Golem patrolled the ghetto, protecting the Jews and catching those responsible for the Blood Libel red-handed. Eventually Rabbi Leow managed to persuade the Emperor to pass laws prohibiting the practice of Blood Libel. Because the Golem was now no longer needed, legend has it that the Rabbi took him up to a room in the loft of the Alt-Neu (Old-New) Synagogue in Prague, removed the paper from his mouth, and he became a lifeless lump of clay. It is said that in a locked room above the synagogue the remains still lie.

Above: *The golem was seen as protector rather than monster.*

Below: *The letter Zayzin.*

Above: *(From right): the letters Ayin, Pei, and Tzaddi.*

This legend was told to me by my father, but there are many different versions that have been handed down orally. In some, the letters SH-E-M are written on the forehead of the Golem, and in order to destroy him one must rub out the middle letter, while in other versions the written words are placed in the Golem's ear and can be removed when necessary.

There are older, less well-known stories, often related to Rabbi Elijah of Chelm, whereby the Golem grew larger and more powerful every day and had to be destroyed, illustrating how the unrestrained power of the elements can bring about havoc and destruction. In this case, the magical word inscribed on the Golem's forehead is said to have been the Hebrew word for truth, *emet* (spelt Aleph/Mem/Tav), and to kill the Golem you had to erase the first letter, Aleph, from his forehead, leaving only *met*—meaning dead.

One of the stories attributed to Rabbi Elijah was that he became frightened because of how large and powerful the Golem had become, but because the Golem had grown so tall the Rabbi was unable to reach his forehead to erase the letter Aleph. He therefore decided to trick the Golem. While sitting down, the Rabbi asked the Golem to pull off his boots. As the Golem bent over to perform this task, the Rabbi was able to reach out and erase the Aleph. However, the Golem immediately became lifeless and fell, and the weight of his body killed the Rabbi, who was seated beneath it.

During the Second World War the legend of the Golem again cropped up, when it is said that it protected the safety of the Alt-Neu Synagogue in Prague. The Germans, who were in occupation, decided to destroy the synagogue, but when they went to do so they heard the steps of a giant walking on the roof, and saw the shadow of a giant hand falling from the window onto the floor. This terrified them, and they fled in panic. One could logically say that the ancient synagogue echoed every sound, and that the ancient glass window panes would distort every shadow, but on the other hand, it is considered miraculous that the Germans left this particular synagogue standing.

Above: *The letter Samekh.*

As with many legends, one must look beyond the fairy tale and seek out the source and facts behind the stories. Many Kabbalists agree that the recipe for formulating a golem is to be found in the *Sepher Yetzirah*, the *Book of Creation*. Some argue that the recipe includes a combination of Hebrew letter magic together with ritual, which would produce within the practitioner an ecstatic state of consciousness that would make them feel that the Golem lived. However, this sublime experience would only last as long as the ecstasy of its creator. Others, however, take this further by stating that once a conceptual golem was formed mentally, this essence could then be transferred to a clay form that could actually be animated. It was through this process that a physical golem could be brought to life.

Whatever theory one believes, it is a matter of record that the Maharal entered a ban on anyone entering the attic of the Alt-Neu Synagogue in Prague, which is still in force today. And it is believed that the body of his Golem rests here until one day it will be called into service again to protect the Jews of Prague.

SEXUAL MAGIC AND THE KABBALAH

I will sing the song of all songs to Solomon that he may smother me with kisses.
Your love is more fragrant than wine, fragrant is the scent of your perfume, and your name like perfume poured out; for this the maidens love you.
Take me with you, and we will run together. You have brought me into your chamber, O king.

THE SONG OF SONGS 1:1–4

T HE MOST FAMOUS piece of Jewish erotic poetry is the "Shir ha-Shirim", "The Song of Songs", written by King Solomon in the Bible. The *Talmud* calls this love song between a man and a woman the "Holy of Holies"—the most sacred biblical text, the reason being that sex is an expression of our deep desire for the ultimate unity—to connect with God. The verse "I am my beloved's and my beloved is mine" (The Song of Songs 6:3) symbolically refers to the longing for oneness with God.

Kabbalah teaches that at the moment of sexual union the female side of God is present over the marital bed. It is taught that because God has female and male personae, and because they are united in perfect harmony, a man must also reenact this in life by having sex with only one woman—his wife. Accordingly, it is taught that a man or woman who has never had sex with a member of the opposite sex can never truly communicate with God.

Because of the sanctity of a loving sexual union, sex without love is an abhorrence to Kabbalists, and therefore only in the marital bed can man reach the divine. In fact, the Hebrew word for the marriage ceremony, *kiddushin*, comes from the word *kodosh*, meaning "holy."

According to the *Zohar* (343b), the souls of a truly matched couple are derived from the common soul-essence. These two souls are destined before birth to unite in matrimony. In order to find a true soul-mate, one

Top left: *The letter Nun.*
Below: *Mem.*

143

must first "find oneself" through studying Kabbalah and learning to live a selfless life.

Certain sexual techniques are taught in Kabbalah that will prolong sexual union, in order to transcend earthly pleasure into higher states of spiritual consciousness. A man and wife should firstly see each other as the personification of the divine image, and this then evolves into the sexual act becoming something holy.

When a man and wife are intimate, the man should think of himself as being filled with the male aspect of God having intimate relations with the female aspect. In the same vein, the woman should think of herself as being the female aspect of God having intimate relations with the male aspect. Together they should both realize that through their sexual coupling, they are creating an "image of God."

It is very important that in order to achieve this higher aspect of sexual union, both partners should not think of any other members of the opposite sex other than the partner that they are actually with. Both should totally focus, as with meditation, upon being totally absorbed with only thoughts of each other, pushing all extraneous thoughts out of their minds.

There are several guidelines found in Kabbalah to transcend the physical pleasures of sex and enter into the state of spiritual ecstasy. These are mainly to enhance the meditative state. It is recommended that the act should take place in a dark room, because the experience should primarily be tactile, using the sense of touch with nothing else to distract each of the partners. In Genesis, we are told of man and woman becoming "one flesh," which indicates that no clothing should come between man and woman, thus maximizing the tactile experience.

Kabbalah teaches that the sexual act should commence with words of love leading to kissing, hugging, and cuddling, eventually leading to full sexual relations. In other words, the speech and kissing begin the process in your head and mind, leading to the fuller feelings of touching and cuddling in your body. This then progresses to the feeling of pleasure in your reproductive organs, which leads in turn to the point of heightened sexual ecstasy. Thus you are controlling the flow of your sexual energy through your mind into your body via your head and spine, filling every part of your body.

Above: *The letter Resh and (left), Shin.*
Opposite: *The letter Tav.*

> **May I find your breasts like clusters of grapes on the vine.**
> **The scent of your breath like apples, and your mouth like spiced wine**
> **flowing smoothly so welcome my caresses, gliding down through lips**
> **and teeth.**
> **I am my beloved's, his longing is all for me.**
> **Come, my beloved, let us go out into the fields to lie among the henna-**
> **bushes; let us go early to the vineyards and see if the vine has budded**
> **or its blossom opened, if the pomegranates are in flower.**
> **There will I give you my love, when the mandrakes give their perfume,**
> **and all rare fruits are ready at our door, fruits new and old which I have**
> **in store for you, my love.**
> THE SONG OF SONGS 7:8–13

THE ACT OF SEXUAL INTIMACY is one of the greatest pleasures that we can experience, and although on the one hand we know that this is because we need to enjoy it in order to procreate, on the other hand, and on a higher spiritual level, it is because it allows a man and a woman to join together to emulate God.

The joy and pleasure of sex will be multiplied if looked upon as a meditative experience, where the man and woman have not only had an intimate fulfillment that can be thought upon as a gift from God, but also realize that at that special moment of ecstasy they have united with the source of creation.

The Torah tells us that a married man must not "diminish his wife's conjugal rights" (Exodus 21:10) which is interpreted in the *Talmud* to mean that it is one of God's commandments that husband and wife have regular sexual intercourse. The best time for sex is on the night of the Sabbath (Friday), and Kabbalists are encouraged to refrain on other nights and conserve their energies for study. The Sabbath is the time to welcome the Sabbath bride, and ideally intimacy should take place after midnight. This is considered the holiest hour, and sex is seen as a sacred act in its own right.

Below: *The letter Kuf.*

> **No other moment is like the ecstasy of the moment when spirit cleaves to spirit in a kiss.**
>
> *ZOHAR* 2:146A

K ABBALAH ENCOURAGES COUPLES to use meditative technique not only to enhance the pleasure experienced, but also to focus their minds on their partners, which will result in strengthening their marriage.

יֹאמְרוּ הַגּוֹיִם אַיֵּה־נָא אֱלֹהֵיהֶם: וֵאלֹהֵינוּ בַשָּׁמָיִם כֹּל אֲשֶׁר־חָפֵץ
עָשָׂה: עֲצַבֵּיהֶם כֶּסֶף וְזָהָב מַעֲשֵׂה יְדֵי אָדָם: פֶּה־לָהֶם וְלֹא יְדַבֵּרוּ עֵינַיִם
לָהֶם וְלֹא יִרְאוּ: אָזְנַיִם לָהֶם וְלֹא יִשְׁמָעוּ אַף לָהֶם וְלֹא יְרִיחוּן: יְדֵיהֶם
וְלֹא יְמִישׁוּן רַגְלֵיהֶם וְלֹא יְהַלֵּכוּ לֹא־יֶהְגּוּ בִּגְרוֹנָם: כְּמוֹהֶם יִהְיוּ עֹשֵׂיהֶם
כֹּל אֲשֶׁר־בֹּטֵחַ בָּהֶם: יִשְׂרָאֵל בְּטַח בַּיְיָ עֶזְרָם וּמָגִנָּם הוּא: בֵּית אַהֲרֹן
בִּטְחוּ בַיְיָ עֶזְרָם וּמָגִנָּם הוּא: יִרְאֵי יְיָ בִּטְחוּ בַיְיָ עֶזְרָם וּמָגִנָּם הוּא:
יְיָ זְכָרָנוּ יְבָרֵךְ יְבָרֵךְ אֶת־בֵּית יִשְׂרָאֵל יְבָרֵךְ אֶת־בֵּית אַהֲרֹן: יְבָרֵךְ
יִרְאֵי יְיָ הַקְּטַנִּים עִם־הַגְּדֹלִים: יֹסֵף יְיָ עֲלֵיכֶם וְעַל־בְּנֵיכֶם:
בְּרוּכִים אַתֶּם לַיְיָ עֹשֵׂה שָׁמַיִם וָאָרֶץ: הַשָּׁמַיִם שָׁמַיִם לַיְיָ וְהָאָרֶץ נָתַן
לִבְנֵי־אָדָם: לֹא הַמֵּתִים יְהַלְלוּ־יָהּ וְלֹא כָּל־יֹרְדֵי דוּמָה: וַאֲנַחְנוּ נְבָרֵךְ

kABBALAH AND THE POWER OF THE HEBREW ALPHABET

KABBALAH AND THE POWER OF THE HEBREW ALPHABET

THE HEBREW ALPHABET represents the forces of creation and was in existence before creation in another dimension, in a state of pure energy. The individual letters, their names, graphic forms, Gemetria (numerical equivalents), sounds, and respective positions are the physical manifestation of translating God's divine power and wisdom into physical reality. They are the transfer of spirituality into physical form.

> The twenty-two sounds and letters are the Foundation of all things.
> He hath formed, weighed, and composed with these twenty-two letters every soul,
> and the soul of everything which shall hereafter be.
>
> *SEPHER YETZIRAH*

THE HEBREW LETTERS connect us to the spiritual realms via their shape, sound frequencies, and vibrations. By making visual contact with the letters and by vocalizing them, a connection is made with the letters that are within our soul (our spiritual DNA). This in turn connects us with the original twenty-two forces of creation—the cosmic DNA.

Through meditation and visual connection to the different energy levels of the letters and the names of God as written in Hebrew, spiritual energy can be transferred to us, giving us the power to help heal our physical, mental, and spiritual bodies, and to effect change within our lives.

Above: *(From right) Resh, Hei, and Vav.*
Below: *Gimel.*

A BRIEF INTRODUCTION

THE HEBREW ALPHABET contains twenty-two letters, all of which are consonants except the first one—Aleph—which may be used as a vowel. Originally Hebrew was written without vowels, but today Hebrew is nearly always written outside Israel with vowel insertions to make it easier to read. Hebrew is read from right to left.

Every Hebrew letter possesses a numerical value, and the study of this in relation to Numerology is called Gemetria. By calculating the numerical equivalence of letters, words, or phrases, and by contemplating upon them through Kabbalah, one can gain insight into different concepts. Certain letters have two values, depending on whether the letter is used within or at the end of a word, i.e. a final letter.

The basic concept underlying Gemetria is that all things have a unique vibration. And therefore numbers, which are represented by the Hebrew alphabet, each have an individual vibrational level that can affect the world around us. An example of this is in the "What's in a Name" in Chapter 1, where the numerical value of the Hebrew letters in one's name can have an effect on one's life. Bearing this in mind, the entire Bible can be viewed as a series of numbers through which the Kabbalist can seek to unfold layer upon layer of hidden meanings.

The following chart shows the Hebrew letter, its name, associated number, and traditional Rabbinical pictographic definitions.

KABBALIST ALPHABET

WITH ITS ASSOCIATED NUMBERS, TRADITIONAL RABBINICAL PICTOGRAPHIC DEFINITIONS, AND TREE OF LIFE PATHWAYS

LETTER	NAME	NUMBER	DEFINITION	PATHWAY
	ALEPH	1	OX	11
	BEIT	2	HOUSE	12
	GIMEL	3	CAMEL	13
	DALED	4	DOOR	14
	HEI	5	WINDOW	15
	VAV	6	NAIL	16
	ZAYIN	7	SWORD	17
	CHET	8	FENCE	18
	TET	9	SERPENT	19
	YOD	10	OPEN HAND	20
	KAPH	20, 500	CLOSED HAND	21
	LAMED	30	OX GOAD (WHIP)	22
	MEM	40, 600	WATER	23
	NUN	50, 700	FISH	24
	SAMEKH	60	PROP	25
	AYIN	70	EYE	26
	PEI	80, 800	MOUTH	27
	TZADDI	90, 900	FISH HOOK	28
	KUF	100	BACK OF HEAD	29
	RESH	200	HEAD	30
	SHIN	300	TOOTH	31
	TAV	400	CROSS	32

THE INDIVIDUAL POWER OF THE HEBREW LETTERS

ALEPH

The numerical value of Aleph is one, and this represents the unique and indivisible God. The energy represented in Aleph is that of the primal force of Creation. Meditate upon Aleph when you are seeking stamina and strength. This will also help you to become more receptive to ideas and creativity.

BEIT

Beit is usually associated with a house (*bayit*), encouraging us to find peace within our own household. It also helps us to understand that we each have our own place within the cosmos, and that God dwells within each of us. Meditate upon Beit when you need to feel at peace, and at home with the world.

GIMEL

Gimel is seen as a kind man running to a needy person, reflecting kindness and growth. Meditate upon Gimel for growth in all aspects of life.

DALED

Daled is the representative of the Four Worlds. It is through these worlds that everything in our physical world has reached us from the point of Creation. Daled is also the beginning of the Hebrew word for doorway (*delet*) and knowledge (*daat*). We are surrounded by hidden doorways in life, and we must learn to tune into our spiritual selves, our sixth sense, to be able to see what we are missing. You can meditate upon Daled in order to open yourself up to the hidden spiritual doorways in your life.

HEI

The letter Hei is found twice in the Tetragrammaton, the sacred name of God: YOD HEI VOV HEI. Its sound resonates as an exhalation of breath, teaching us that it is important to focus on breathing when searching for spiritual advancement. A clear example of this is that most forms of meditative work begin with a simple breathing exercise. Hei also represents the number five, which alludes to the five dimensions of the human soul: *nefesh*, physical intuition; *ruach*, emotions; *neshamah*, mentality;

chayah, spiritual awareness; and *yechidah*, or unity with God. You can meditate upon the letter Hei as a part of your quest for spiritual advancement in the spiritual realms.

VAV

The shape of Vav, like a pillar standing alone, signifies that each person is unique and that every existence is meaningful.

You can meditate on the letter Vav as part of revealing your inner uniqueness to the world, in order that you can strengthen your social connection with others.

ZAYIN

Zayin represents the number seven, the number of completion and unity—the number of days in a week. It also encourages us to remember that it is our soul that is the most important part of our being, and that we should not become too bogged down with banal, everyday matters. You can meditate upon Zayin to become more relaxed and less stressed with everyday living.

CHET

Chet is the first letter of the word *chai*—life—and therefore is important in promoting health and vitality. It also is the first letter of the word *chalom*—dream. Dreams are considered very important channels though which we receive inspiration, warnings, and even spiritual communications.

Meditate upon Chet for physical health. You can also meditate upon Chet if you wish for greater spiritual understanding, or guidance through your dreams.

TET

Tet is the first letter of the Hebrew word *tov*, meaning good, and its shape, with its inwardly curved arm, represents that good is often hidden from us. In Kabbalah goodness is often affiliated with divine light. Tet is also the first letter of the Hebrew word *tahor*, or brilliance and purity. This can illustrate that as we experience spiritual clarity, so our soul will become more open to divine communication. Meditate upon Tet to open up to true goodness and spiritual inspiration.

YOD

This letter represents the number ten, and is linked to the energies of the ten Sephirot on the Tree of Life. This small letter, which seems to hang suspended in the air, represents a spiritual messenger bringing change into our lives. Its small shape contains great energy and force. Meditate on the letter Yod to bring change into your life.

LAMED

Lamed has the numerical value of thirty, and according to mystical tradition, in every generation there are thirty-six—*lamed-vov*—truly righteous people on earth. Meditate upon the letter Lamed while asking how you can become a truly righteous person.

KAPH

Kaph is the first letter of the Hebrew word *kavannah*, which describes intention, willpower, and single-mindedness. *Kavannah* is considered one of the primary keys to transcendental awareness through meditation, prayer, and the visual forms of the Hebrew alphabet. Meditate on the letter Kaph to improve your willpower.

MEM

Mem is the first letter of the Hebrew word *maggid*, which is used to describe a learned teacher, and also a spirit guide. Learning Kabbalah is about attaining a higher spiritual level, allowing us to connect with our spiritual guides. Mem is also the first letter of *molech*—angel. Many people are now aware of the angelic energies that surround us and are waiting to enter our lives. Meditate upon the letter Mem to open yourself up to your angels and spiritual guides.

NUN

Nun is the Aramaic word for fish, which denotes abundance and fertility. This suggests that faith and understanding can bring a feeling of great affluence into our lives. Nun also has the twofold meaning of regeneration and disintegration, making one aware of life's natural cycles, such as birth, growth, and decline.

Meditate upon the letter Nun in order to strengthen your faith, and also to think about your true identity.

SAMEKH

The sealed form of Samekh represents completion. This makes us think about the power that is within each and every one of us to make both our lives and the lives of those around us better. It also symbolizes how God protects each and every one of us.

Meditate on the letter Samekh to become aware of your inner strength, and also to let the divine energy of God protect you.

AYIN

Ayin begins the Hebrew word for eyes—*aynayim*—and teaches us to open up our eyes more fully to the world around us. Kabbalah teaches us that we go around with blinkered vision, and it is up to us to develop and grow spiritually in order to see more clearly the world around us. Ayin also begins the word *aytz*—tree—which brings to mind that we are all part of the Tree of Life, which is filled with the divine light of God.

Meditate on the letter Ayin to open up your eyes and heart to the world around you, enhancing your insight and intuition in everything that you do.

PEI

Pei begins the Hebrew word for mouth—*peh*—and is therefore seen to represent the power that speech and sound can make. Not only is it one of the fundamental bases of human connection, but by resonating correctly the names of God it can add an extra dimension to the power of healing.

Meditate on the letter Pei to enhance your communication with your fellow man.

TZADDI

Tzaddi is the first letter of the Hebrew word *tzadik*, which means righteous. *Tzaddikim* have always been revered in their communities for their sense of community, goodness, and spirituality.

Meditate upon the letter Tzaddi to enhance your feeling of goodwill to your fellow man.

KUF

Kuf begins the word *kaba*, to receive, which is the root word of Kabbalah. By opening ourselves up to receiving the knowledge of Kabbalah, we are entering a new state of spiritual knowledge and awareness.

Meditate upon the letter Kuf to increase your spiritual awareness and knowledge.

RESH

Resh begins the Hebrew word for the holy spirit—*ruach ha-kadosh*—and therefore our ability to transcend spiritually. It is through this

that we can greatly enhance our senses as we open up to intuition and to becoming an open channel to the spiritual world. It is through this channel that spiritual guides allow spiritual healers and teachers to carry out their work here on earth.

Meditate on the letter Resh to enhance your senses and intuition.

SHIN

This is the first letter of the Hebrew word *shalom*, meaning peace. It is the first letter of *Shabbat*, which means a time of harmonious rest and reflection. It is also the first letter of the word *shana*, meaning year, which can lead us to meditate on how we should achieve greater knowledge and spirituality with each progressing year of our lives.

Meditate on the letter Shin to bring peace and harmony into your life.

TAV

The twenty-second and final letter of the Hebrew alphabet is Tav, symbolizing that our lives are a cycle which, when it has been completed, marks another phase in the spiritual learning journey of our souls.

Meditate on the letter Tav to understand the meaning of your life and the lessons you are continuing to learn.

Glossary

PEOPLE

MOSHE BEN NACHMAN 1194–1270

Known better as Nachmanides or Ramban, he was a Spaniard who was both a physician and a scholar with a strong mystical bent. His biblical commentaries are the first ones to incorporate the mystical teachings of Kabbalah.

MOSES DE LEON C. 1240–1305

First publisher of the *Sepher Zohar*. Although he accredited authorship to Simeon Bar Yochai, many believe that much may be original to Moses de Leon and his followers.

MOSES CORDEVERO 1522–70

Known as the Ramak, he was a philosopher, scholar, and Kabbalist based in Safed. He rationally systematized all of Kabbalist thought up to his time, in particular the teachings of the *Zohar*.

ISAAC BEN SOLOMON LURIA 1534–72

Also known as the Ari and Isaac Ashkenazi, Luria revolutionized the study of Kabbalah. He created the idea of *zimzum*, the belief that God in a way "shrunk Himself" to create a void in which to form the world. He could see people's sins by looking at their foreheads, and taught methods to communicate with the souls of *tzaddikim* (righteous people).

CHAIM VITAL 1543–1620

The leading disciple of Rabbi Isaac Luria. Originally studied Kabbalah under Rabbi Moses Cordevero, but later become devoted to the Ari.

SHABBETAI TZVI 1626–76

A Turkish Jew who announced he was the Messiah, and whose chief spokesman was Nathan of Gaza. He had followers all over the world, who heeded his call to sell their possessions and travel with him to Israel to rebuild the Temple. When Shabbetai and his followers reached Constantinople, the Sultan, fearing an uprising, imprisoned Shabbetai, who was offered the choice between death and conversion to Islam. He chose conversion. His followers were called Sabbatians.

ISRAEL BEN ELIEZER C. 1700-1760

Founder of the Hassidic movement. Also known as the Baal Shem Tov, or Besht, he won the respect of unlearned Jews by teaching them that they could see God in everything, by exercising sincere devotion in prayer accompanied by singing, dancing, movement, and storytelling. With time, the Hassidim have toned down their ecstatic and meditative practices, but it is primarily this movement that has kept alive the knowledge and practice of Kabbalah.

GERSHOM SCHOLEM 1897–1982

Professor of Jewish Mysticism at the Hebrew University, Jerusalem. His well-known books include *Major Trends in Jewish Mysticism*, *The Zohar*, and *On the Mystical Shape of the Godhead: Basic Concepts in the Kabbalah*.

ARYEH KAPLAN 1934–83

A traditional, Orthodox Rabbi who spent the 1970s and 1980s reconstructing forgotten traditions of Jewish meditation by researching long-neglected Kabbalist manuscripts. He wrote over fifty books before his untimely death at the age of forty-eight.

SOURCE BOOKS

THE MIDRASH

These books contain interpretation and elaboration on scriptural text. They also contain Halakhic (legal) and Haggadic (non-legal) materials derived from the Hebrew Bible.

THE MISHNAH

The oldest post-biblical collection and codification of Jewish oral laws, organized by various scholars into their final form early in 3 CE by Judah ha-Nasi. The *Mishnah* expands upon the laws found in the Pentateuch—The Five Books of Moses—and includes the various interpretations of legal laws that had been orally preserved since at least the period of Ezra (*c.* 450 BCE).

THE PENTATEUCH

The first five books of the Hebrew Bible, also known as The Five Books of Moses.

SEPHER YETZIRAH (THE BOOK OF CREATION OR THE FORMATION)

It is believed by many that Adam and Noah were aware of the oral laws contained within this ancient manuscript, which were passed down from mouth to ear until Abraham wrote the book at the age of forty-eight, when he converted from idol worship to the religion of the One True God. It has been likened by many to containing the building blocks of all existence, using the combinations of the twenty-two letters of the Hebrew alphabet as its basic units. It can be used as a source of meditation and spirituality, and also it would seem to have been used as the source of creating artificial life—golems.

THE TALMUD

This contains interpretations of the *Mishnah* by two different groups of scholars. The Babylonian *Talmud* (*Talmud Bavli*) is more extensive than the Jerusalem *Talmud* (*Talmud Yerushalmi*), although neither completely cover the entire *Mishnah*. The *Talmud* not only contains legal laws but also discourses, ideas, and discussions on many areas of human interest.

THE TORAH

This is most often taken to mean the first five books of the Old Testament, also called The Five Books of Moses, or the Pentateuch. In fact, the term Torah is also used to cover the whole Hebrew Bible and the written laws contained therein (also known as the Tanakh), and the oral law.

THE ZOHAR (THE BOOK OF SPLENDOR)

Considered by many to be the most important literary work of the Kabbalah the *Zohar* was published by Rabbi Moses de Leon in Guadalajara, Spain, in the thirteenth century. Many believe that Moses de Leon was the original author, although he credited the second-century Galilean sage Simeon Bar Yochai with its authorship.

The *Zohar* explains Kabbalah's origins by weaving myth with fiction, often in the form of legends, narratives, and parables. It goes back to the time before the advent of mankind, when Kabbalah was taught by God to the angels, who then passed on its secrets to the first man—Adam. These teachings were then passed on to Noah, and then to Abraham, who took them to Egypt, where they were studied by Moses. It is said that during the Israelites' period of wandering in the desert, Moses spent his time studying Kabbalah with the assistance of an angel. These teachings were then orally transmitted down through a chosen few, including King David and King Solomon, until they were eventually written down.

Bibliography

Fortune, Dion, *The Mystical Qabalah*, Samuel Weisner Inc., York Beach, Maine, 1999

Halevi, Z'ev ben Shimon, *Kabbalah: Tradition of Hidden Knowledge*, Thames and Hudson, New York, 1998

Isaacs, Ronald H., *Divination, Magic and Healing: The Book of Jewish Folklore*, Jason Aronson Inc., Northvale, New Jersey, 1997

Kaplan, Aryeh, *Jewish Meditation*, Schoken Books, New York, 1995

Scholem, Gershom, *Major Trends in Jewish Mysticism*, Schoken Books, New York, 1968

Scholem, Gershom (ed.), *Zohar: The Book of Splendor*, Schoken Books, New York, 1995

Wolf, Rabbi Laibl, *Practical Kabbalah*, Three Rivers Press, New York, 1999

It should also be mentioned that there are many excellent Internet sites on all subjects related to the Kabbalah from all different viewpoints and aspects, as well as many sites on Lilith and the Golem. The problem with giving specific website addresses here, however, is that by the time this book is published, the addresses may not exist any more.

Translations of the *Sepher Yitzerah* can also be found on the Internet.

Acknowledgments

THIS book is the direct result of the knowledge that my late father, Sidney Abraham Pepper, passed on to me to keep alive the mystical oral traditions of Kabbalah, as they had been passed down through untold generations of his family. I am grateful for his wisdom and foresight in passing on this wonderful inheritance.

I am indebted to my husband, Jeffrey, my children, Nicole, Simone, and Alexis, and my mother, Lily Pepper, for their endless encouragement and support for this project, which is the result of my ceaseless journey to expand my knowledge of Kabbalah and spirituality.

A special thanks must go to my great Editor, Liz Dean, who has guided and supported me in writing this book, and to Cindy Richards and the team at Cico Books for their confidence and backing. As always, a big thank you to my literary agent, Chelsey Fox, for all her encouragement, patience and advice.

Index